AF576563

FREDERIC REMINGTON

Masterpieces from the Amon Carter Museum

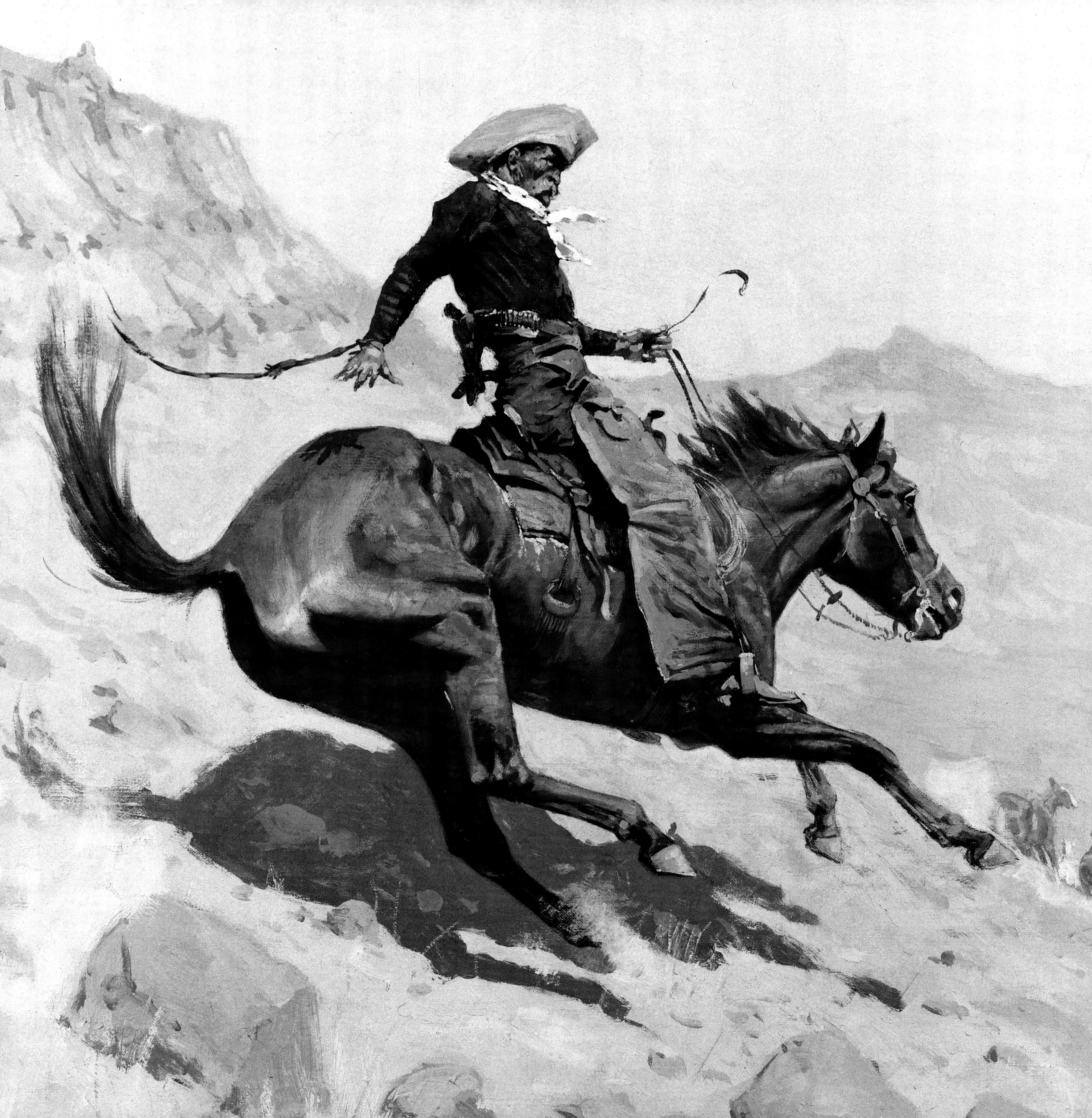

FREDERIC REMINGTON

Masterpieces from the Amon Carter Museum

RICK STEWART

Curator of Western Painting and Sculpture, Amon Carter Museum

AMON CARTER MUSEUM

Fort Worth

Distributed by the Amon Carter Museum, Fort Worth

ISBN 0–88360–072–2
Library of Congress Catalog No. 92–54540

Design by DUO Design Group Inc., Fort Worth, Texas
Color separations by JTM Colorscan, Inc., Fort Worth, Texas
Printing by Jarvis Press, Dallas, Texas

Frontispiece: Detail from *The Cowboy*, 1902, oil on canvas
This page: Photograph by Luther Smith

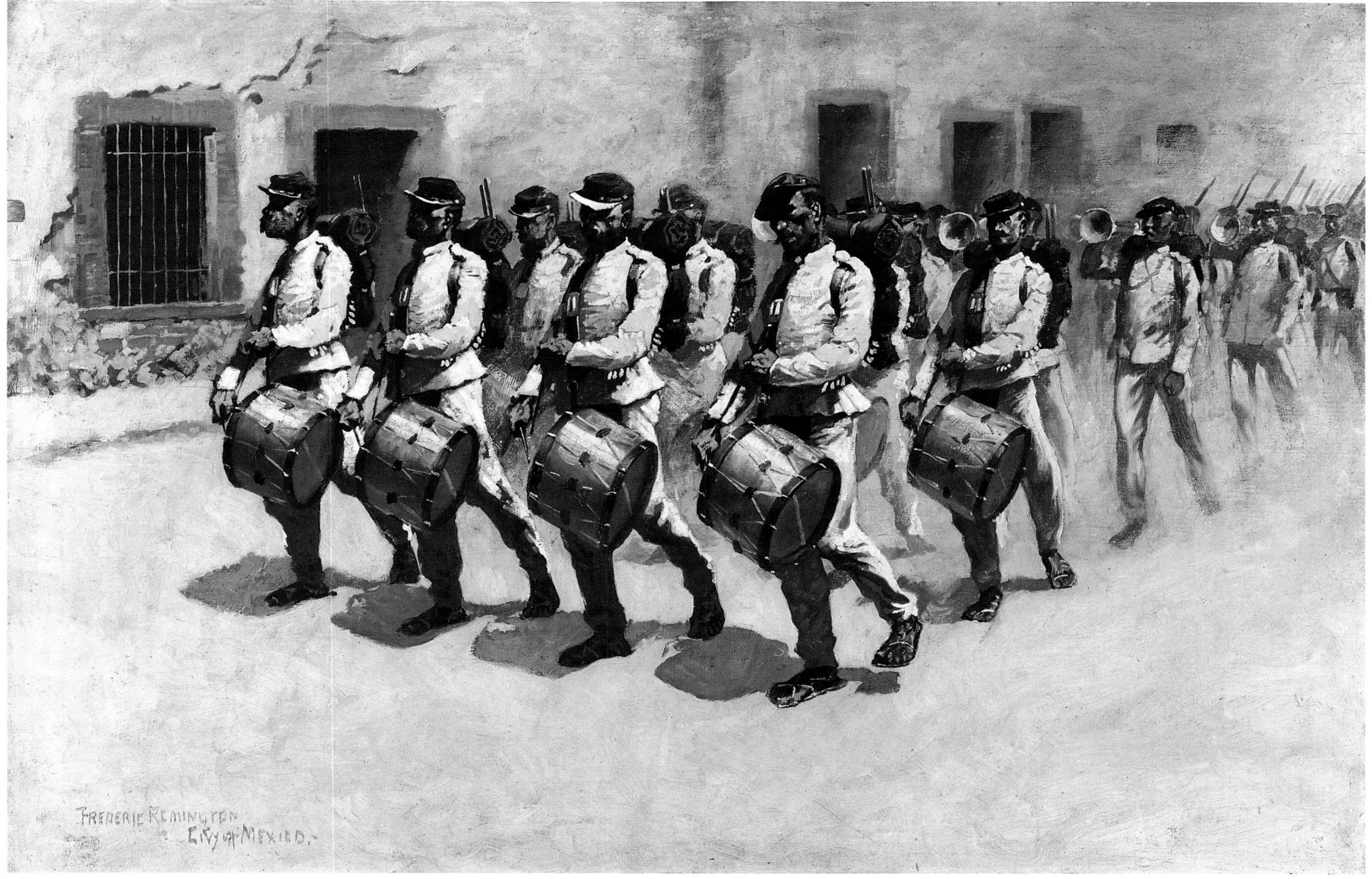

Drum Corps, Mexican Army, 1889, c. 1889, oil on panel

"I regard Frederic Remington as one of the Americans who has done real work for his country, and we all owe him a debt of gratitude." So wrote President Theodore Roosevelt in a letter of tribute published in *Pearson's Magazine* in October 1907. "He has been granted the very unusual gift of excelling in two entirely distinct types of artistic work[,] for his bronzes are as noteworthy as his pictures. He is, of course, one of the most typical American artists we have ever had, and he has portrayed a most characteristic and yet vanishing type of American life. The soldier, the cowboy and rancher, the Indian, the horses and the cattle of the plains, will live in his pictures and bronzes, I verily believe, for all time." This was high praise from one who had made his own considerable contribution to American life, but the two men shared one thing in common: their accomplishments were conditioned by, and based on, their experiences in the American West. Roosevelt wrote a multivolume history titled *The Winning of the West*, in which he viewed the whole process as a conquest that defined the national character. His writings about the West were filled with moral notions of intense experience, manly

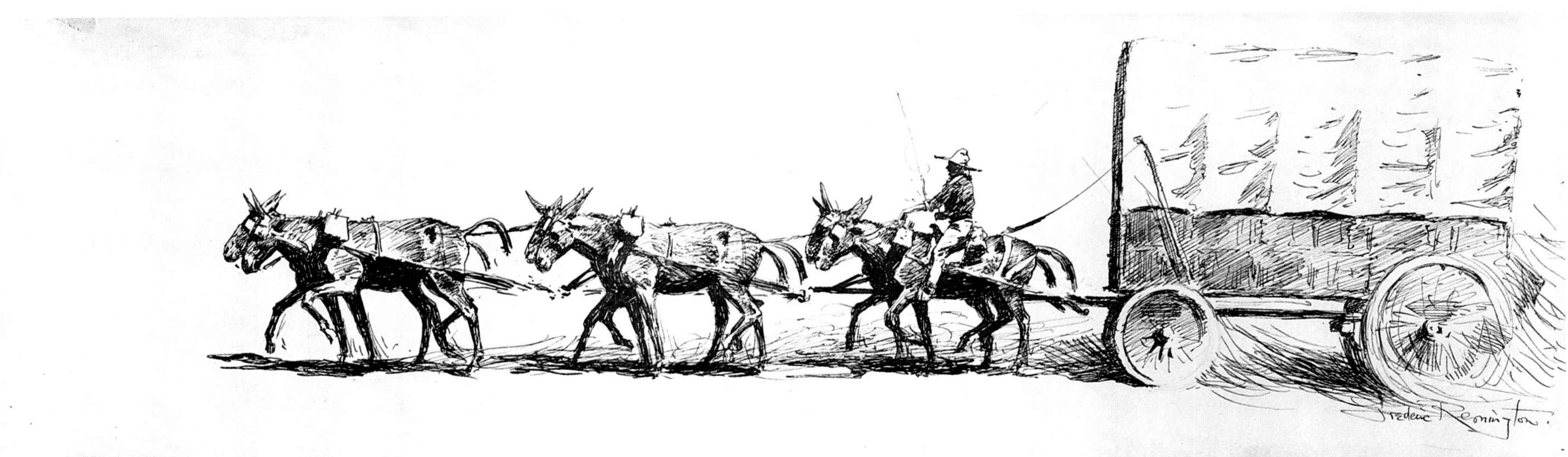

The Old Transcontinental Freighter, 1890, pen and ink on paper

action, fierce emotion, and primitive environments. In this respect he resembled his friend Remington, whose writings and visual works echoed similar themes.

Both Remington and Roosevelt became principal myth-makers for their era, celebrating the West in a way that blurred the distinction between the subjective and objective, the imaginative and the factual. As early as March 1892, a writer for *Scribner's Magazine* understood Remington's achievement. "In his pictures of life on the plains, and of Indian fighting, he has almost created a new field in illustration so fresh and novel are his characterizations, realized as they have never been before," the writer observed. "It is a fact that admits of no question that Eastern people have formed their conceptions of what the Far-Western life is like, more from what they have seen in Mr. Remington's pictures than from any other source, and if they went to the West or Mexico they would expect to see men and places

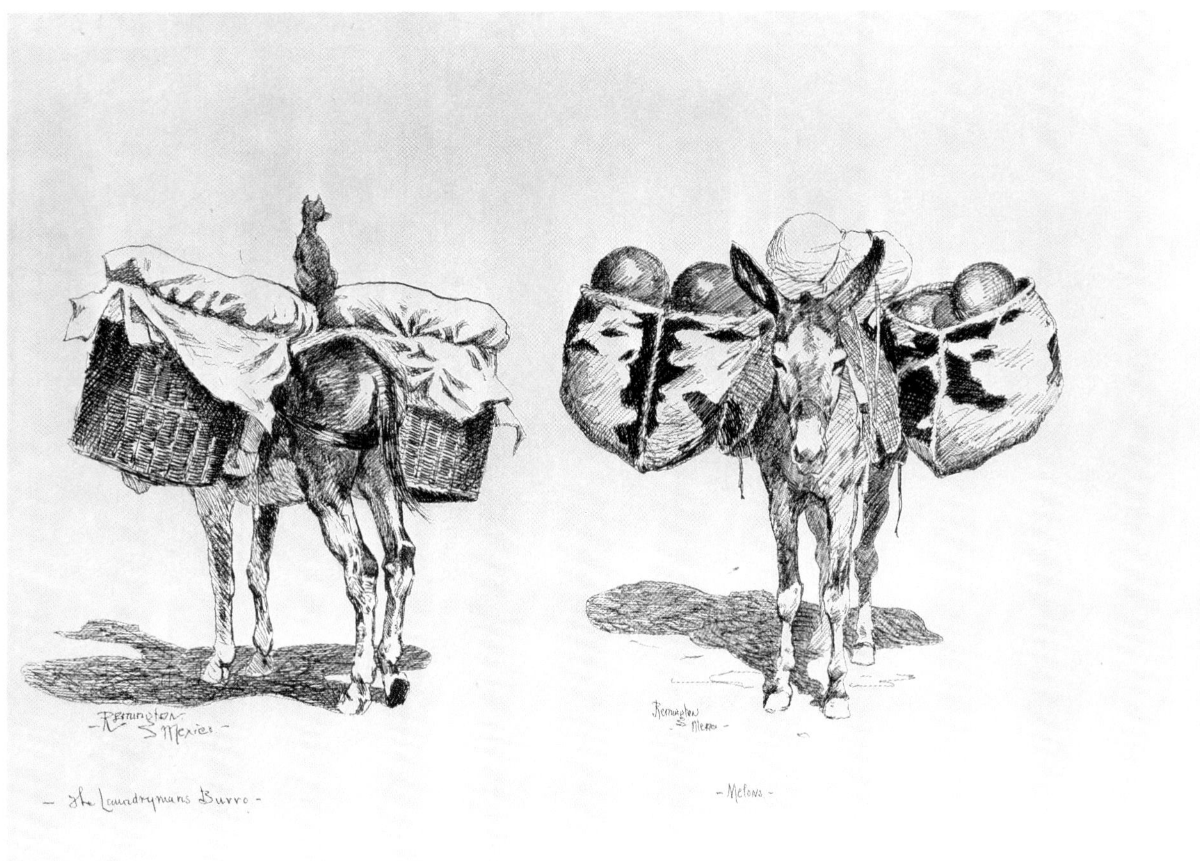

Mexican Burros, 1889, pen and ink on board

looking exactly as Mr. Remington has drawn them." Remington's influence eventually extended to the popular media in general. Scholars have shown, for example, that many of Hollywood's leading motion picture directors, such as John Ford, utilized Remington's visual imagery in their own work. In words that Remington surely would have approved, Ford once told an interviewer that he was concerned in his films with "building fact into legend."

Amon G. Carter, Sr., first heard about the work of Frederic Remington through his friend, the writer and humorist Will Rogers. In 1935, the same year that he began acquiring works by Charles M. Russell, Carter also purchased his first Remington painting, *His First Lesson*, from a New York dealer. From the beginning, Carter's interest in possessing art works by Remington and Russell was predicated upon sharing them with others. The works were placed on the walls of the Fort Worth Club or displayed at the Fort Worth Public Library, both downtown. As his collection grew, Carter often consulted with his friend C. R. Smith, the aviation industry pioneer, about his purchases, and he sought particular advice from Harold McCracken, then the leading expert in the country on Remington's art. "I have been working towards picking up pictures and bronzes from time to time for the purpose of eventually building a Remington and Russell museum," Carter wrote McCracken in May 1949. "This I would like to do while I am around in person and hope to carry the plan through." In July that same year Carter visited the Remington Art Memorial museum in Ogdensburg, New York, and visited with Emma Caten, the artist's sister-in-law. At the time, Carter hoped to be able to acquire

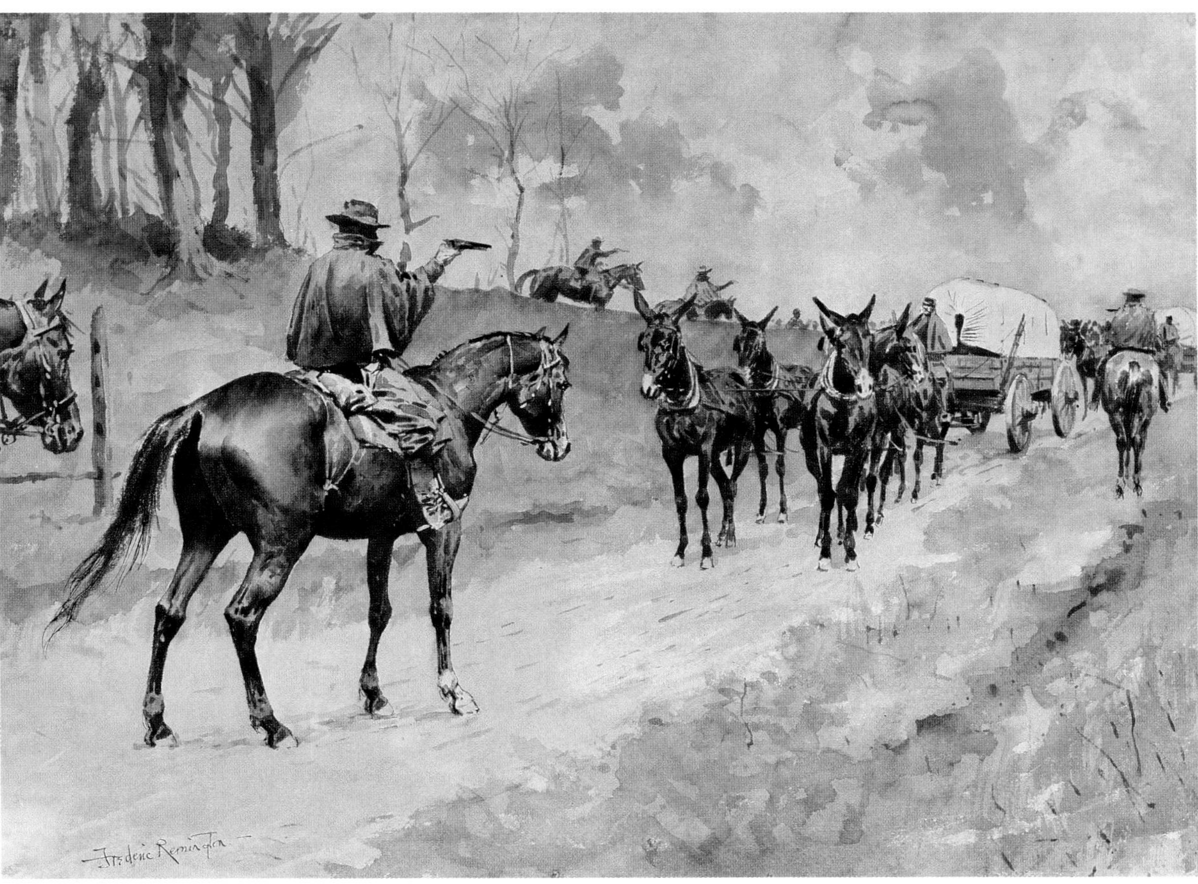

Morgan's Raiders Capturing a Train, c. 1895, ink wash on paper

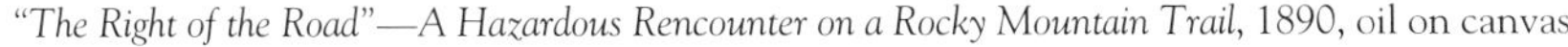

"The Right of the Road"—A Hazardous Rencounter on a Rocky Mountain Trail, 1890, oil on canvas

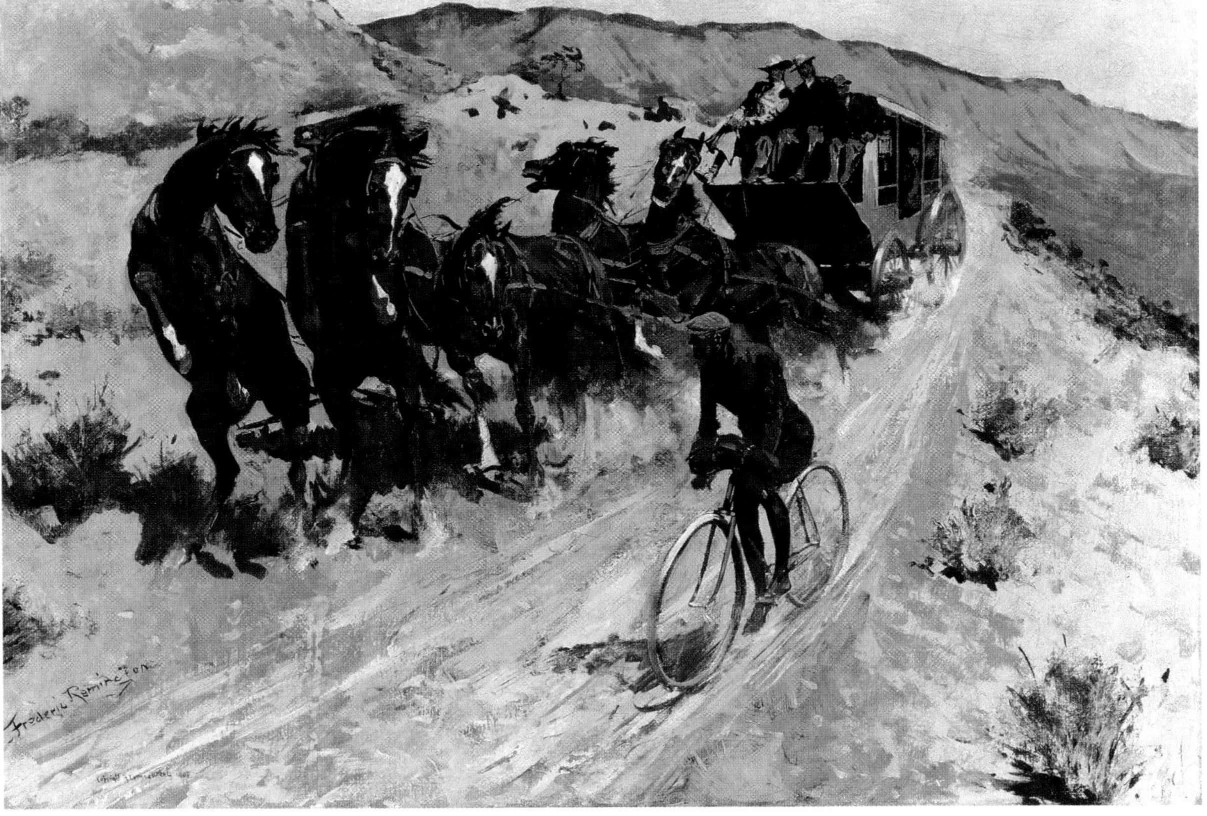

the Ogdensburg collection for his museum in Fort Worth, but he was not successful.

By 1950 Carter acknowledged that he was so busy with numerous projects that he had no time to devote to his plan for a museum. Nevertheless, with the idea of a public collection firmly in his mind and McCracken advising him on several occasions, he continued to add to his Remington holdings. Carter also realized the need to acquire materials that would allow future generations to study the artists and their works, and this foresight led to the purchase of Harry B. Smith's renowned collection of library and archival materials concerning Remington's life and work.

Following Carter's death in 1955, tributes to his generosity and foresight poured in from all quarters, and on January 21, 1961, the Museum that he had envisioned opened its doors to the public. His acclaimed collection of paintings by Charles M. Russell and Frederic Remington was there to be enjoyed by future generations and to pay a lasting homage to the determination and courage of the pioneer spirit. "Amon G. Carter was born and reared in a frontier community," C. R. Smith wrote in the inaugural catalogue. "He acquired there the habits which later brought success to his business life. He also acquired and thereafter maintained a spirit of generosity. He wanted others to do well, he wanted to share with others the opportunities which come to able men."

Her Calf, 1897, pen and ink wash on paper

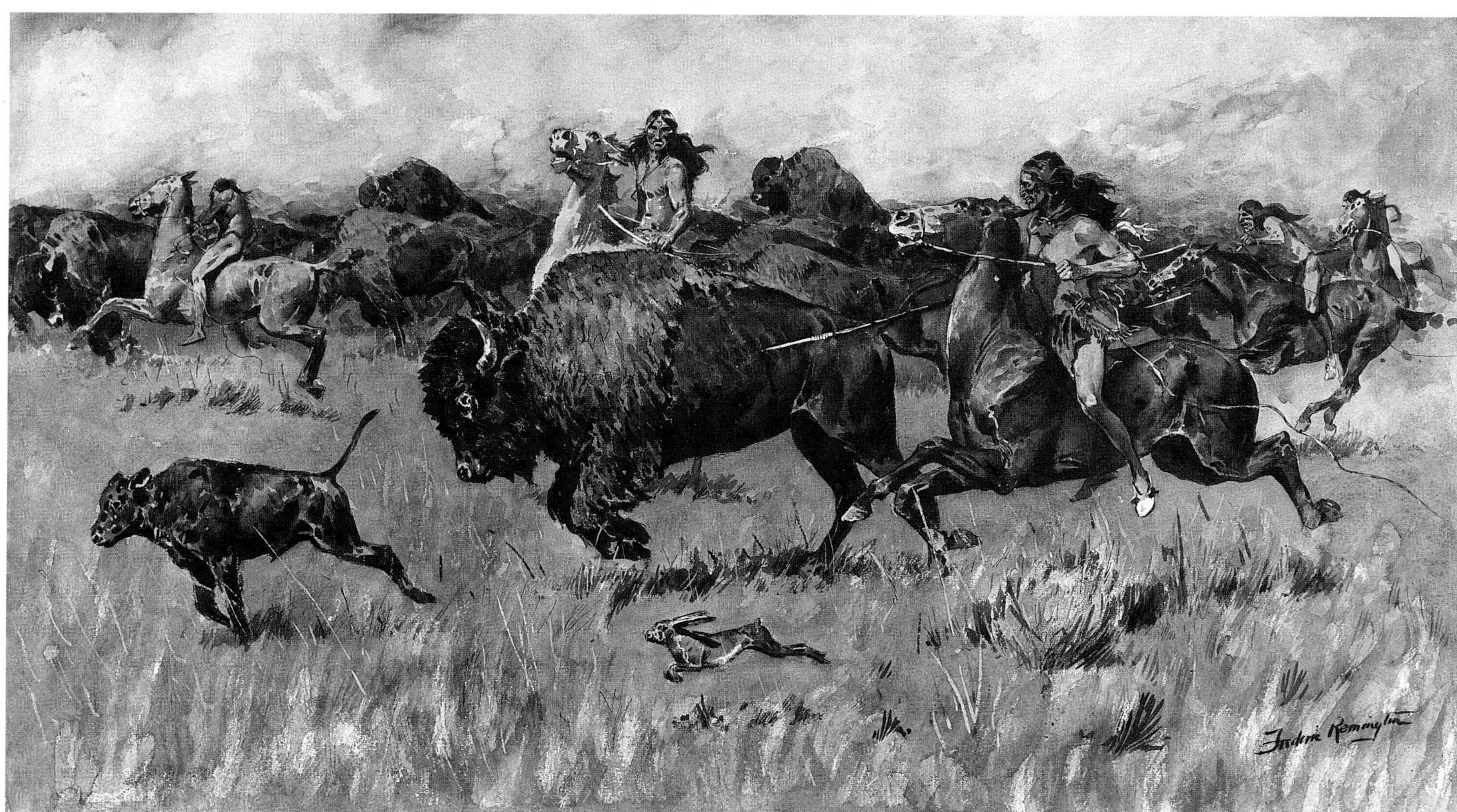

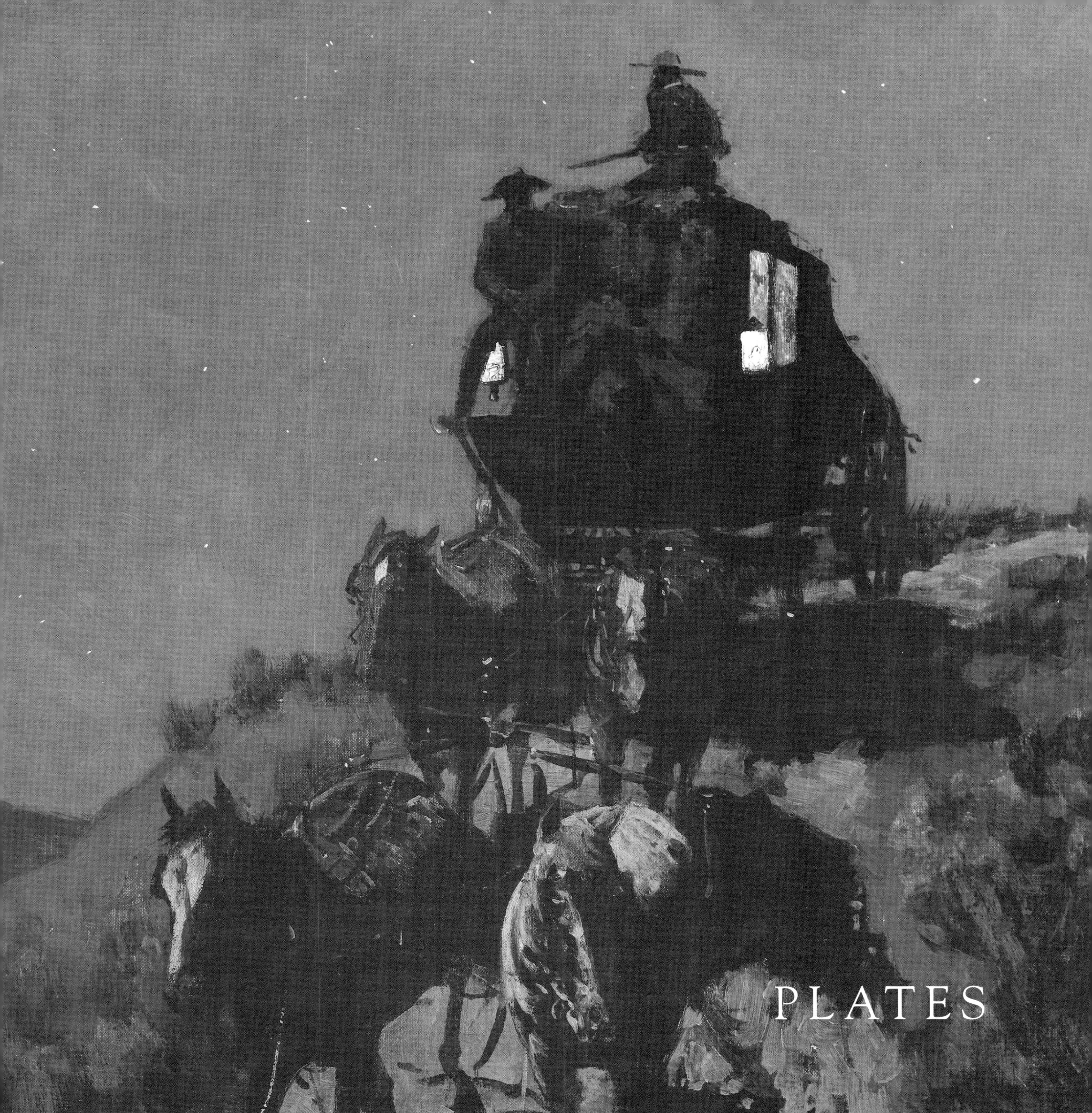

PLATES

A Dash for the Timber

1889, oil on canvas, 48¼ x 84⅛ inches

Frederic Remington (1861–1909), born and raised in upstate New York near the Saint Lawrence River, became one of the most accomplished and influential artists of the American West. Surprisingly, his formal artistic training was limited to three semesters at the Yale College of Art, when he was seventeen, and a three-month stint at the Art Students League in New York eight years later, when his career was just getting under way. He made his first trip to the American West in 1881, vacationing in the Montana Territory, and two years later he moved to Kansas. There he became involved in a series of short-lived ventures that included a sheep ranch, a hardware store, and a saloon. All the while, Remington worked at becoming an artist. Returning to New York City in 1885, he established a working relationship with *Harper's Weekly*, then the largest pictorial newspaper in the world. Remington's rise to prominence was meteoric; within a few years he became one of the best and most prolific artist-correspondents of the era.

Between 1885 and 1888 Remington made a number of trips to the American Southwest, principally to cover the U.S. Cavalry and its pursuit of the Apaches. The stark landscape and dramatic human events he encountered there greatly influenced his artistic development. Remington filled his diaries with observations, made countless field sketches, took many photographs with the latest equipment, and collected numerous artifacts to use in his paintings. "I have a big order for a cowboy picture and I want a lot of 'chapperas'—say two or three pieces—and if you will buy them off some of the cowboys and ship them to me by express c.o.d. I will be your slave," the artist wrote a friend in Arizona in April 1889. "I want *old ones*—and they should all be different in shape. . . . I have four pairs now and want some more and as soon as I can get them will begin the picture."

He was probably referring to *A Dash for the Timber*, which launched his career as a major painter when it was exhibited at the National Academy in 1889. "This work marks an advance on the part of one of the strongest of our younger artists, who is one of the best illustrators we have," praised a writer in the *New York Herald*. "The drawing is true and strong, the figures of men and horses are in fine action, tearing along at full gallop, the sunshine effect is realistic and the color is good." Remington's delineation of the horses is a particular artistic triumph; they charge toward the viewer with nostrils flaring and every muscle strained to its limits. The headlong motion of horses and riders seems suspended above patches of cool purple and blue shadow, contrasting with warmer tones of yellow and orange in the surrounding landscape. The overall effect is cinematic, and this action-filled portrayal of the struggle for life on the frontier anticipates the many western films that were to follow a generation later.

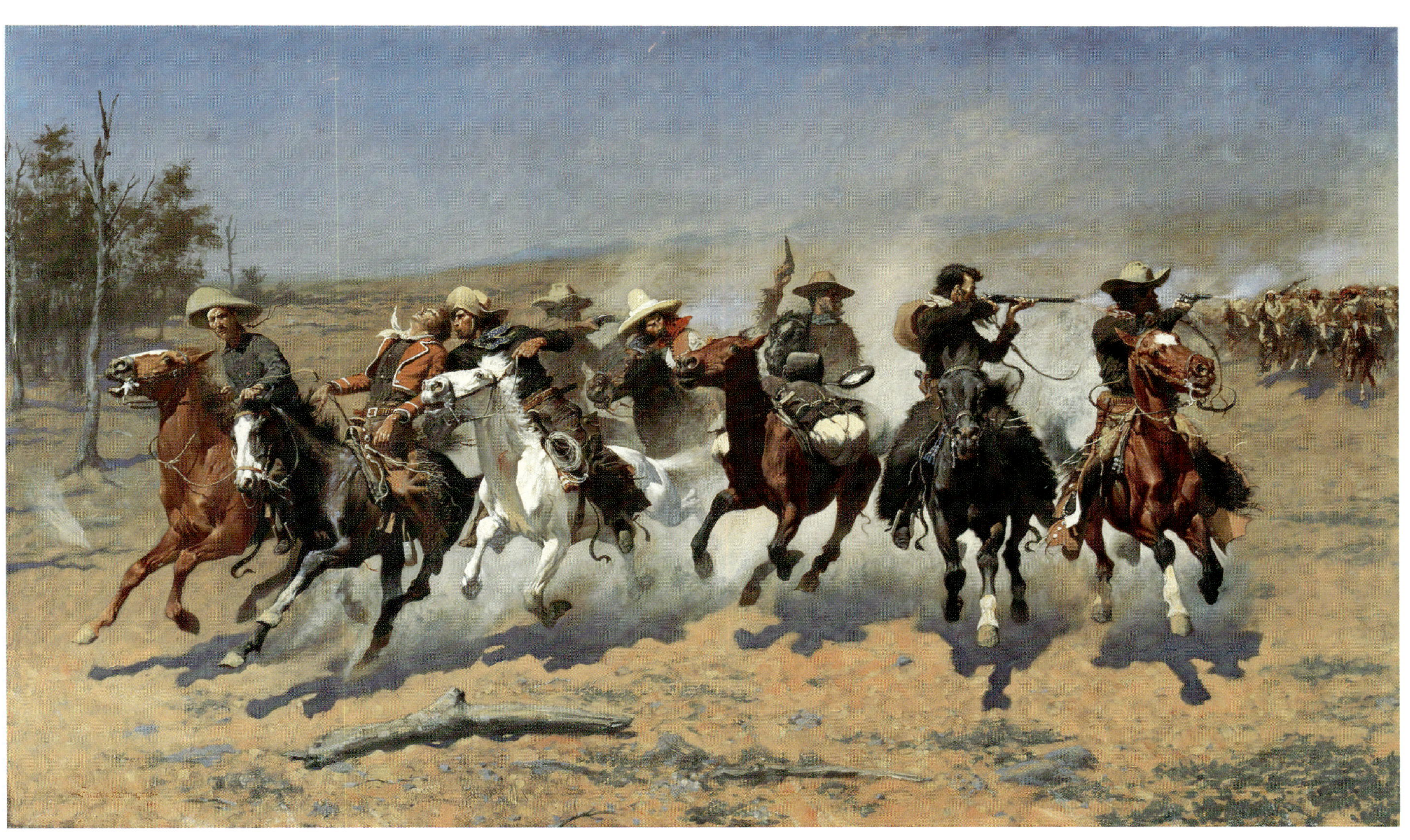

An Indian Trapper

1889, oil on canvas, 49 x 34⅛ inches

In April 1887 Remington persuaded his editors at *Harper's Weekly* to send him on a sketching trip to the Canadian West. He went overland by rail through North Dakota and into Wyoming to spend some time at the Crow Indian Agency, then headed north toward Calgary, Alberta, and the Blackfoot reservation south of the Bow River. He was frustrated to find the Indians hostile to his attempts to sketch them; in his own words, "after a long and tedious course of diplomacy," he was allowed "to get one of these people to gaze in a defiant and fearful way down the mouth of a camera." He persisted, however, and soon had enough material to provide full-page drawings for the magazine for more than six months. Characteristically, the artist was especially interested in Blackfoot dress, weapons, implements, and modes of decoration, such as beadwork—all of it good information for later efforts at his easel, including *An Indian Trapper*, which he completed two years after his return.

Remington's vivid depiction was one of two paintings he exhibited in 1889 at the Brooklyn Art Club, where it quickly sold. The work later illustrated an article by Colonel Theodore A. Dodge, titled "Some American Riders," which appeared in *Harper's New Monthly Magazine* in May 1891. "The Indian trapper whom our artist has depicted may be a Cree, or perhaps a Blackfoot, whom one was apt to run across in the Selkirk Mountains or elsewhere on the plains of the British Territory, or well up north in the Rockies, toward the outbreak of the Civil War," Dodge wrote. "He was tributary to the Hudson's Bay Company, whose badge he wore in his blanket coat of English manufacture, which he had got in trade." The trapper wears fringed leggings and moccasins decorated with ornamental beadwork, as well as a thick animal-fur cap that was typical dress for Blackfeet in the northern climate. A buffalo robe, used for comfort and added warmth, is rolled up behind the Indian's saddle, and a two-bladed "beaver tail" knife in a colorful scabbard can be seen against the red sash on his waist. He grips a tack-studded quirt in his left hand, while cradling a musket that shows the same brass-tack decoration on its stock. The horse is the typically lithe, hammer-headed type that Remington frequently depicted in his works; here, its sleek black coat shimmers in the bright light of the alpine landscape.

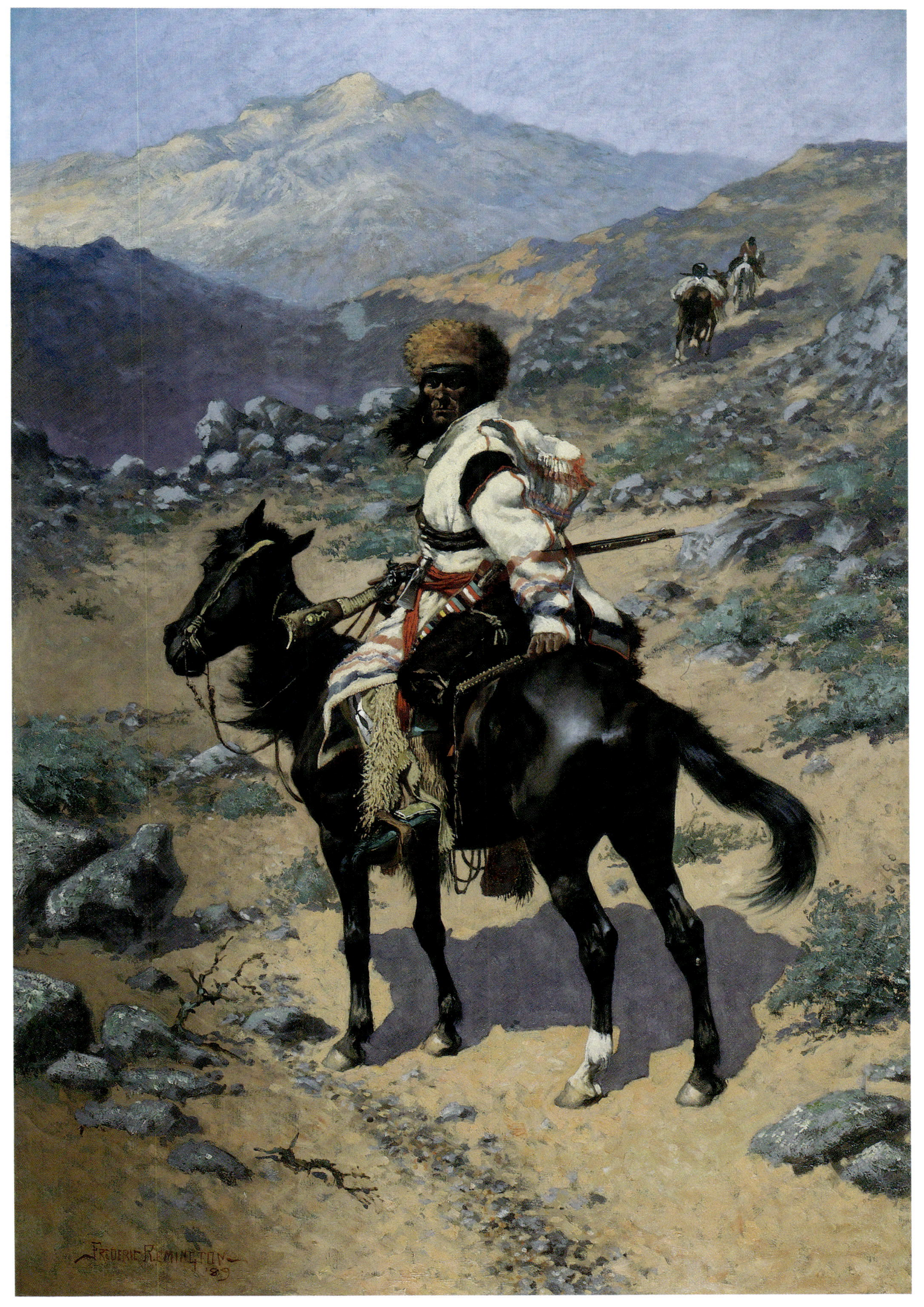
FREDERIC REMINGTON '89

Cavalryman of the Line, Mexico

1889, oil on canvas, 24⅛ x 20 inches

In the April 27, 1889, *Harper's Weekly*, an item in the "Personal" column read: "Frederic Remington during his recent Mexican trip, undertaken in the interests of *Harper's Magazine* and the *Weekly*, had a specimen member of various regiments in the regular army of Mexico under his immediate orders. He was thus enabled, through the courtesy of the Mexican Minister of War, to make a most complete series of military sketches." One of these was the painting reproduced here, a strikingly vivid study of a Mexican army horseman in dress uniform, astride his mount, with a row of military stables in the background.

Remington spent more than six weeks in Mexico gathering material for a series of stories, including one he hoped to write himself. He also asked an army acquaintance in New Mexico for "all the facts concerning the operation of Mex[ican] regular troops in Sonora—their marching and fighting—I may use it." Remington never wrote the article, but fifteen of his works illustrated "The Mexican Army," an overview by Thomas A. Janvier in *Harper's New Monthly Magazine* for November 1889. "As it is today," Janvier wrote, "no longer a confused mass made up of scattered commands faithful only to their respective generals, but an organization loyal to the nation and to the idea of national unity—the Mexican army is an honor to the government that has created it."

The following year an unsigned article in *Harper's Weekly* traced the fortunes of a Mexican cavalry unit in a setting very reminiscent of Remington's painting. "The scene is an arid upland in a white glare of sunlight beneath an unchanging clear blue sky," it began. "In this desert landscape a detachment of Mexican cavalry is drawn up in line ready to set out on a march." The article went on to describe "the strikingly picturesque" figure of a horseman sitting erect in his saddle, "with all the *esprit* of his profession"—a soldier who was not likely to be prevented from "carrying out to the letter the orders of his official superiors or his individual ideas of military duty." These qualities are also evident in Remington's respectful portrayal of the cavalryman, whose unit was efficient enough to be a dreaded enemy even to the skilled Apaches. Remington's depiction of the dappled horse in this painting is particularly accomplished, the result of much careful study in the field. Mexican cavalry horses were smaller than their Kentucky counterparts, but "wiry, fleet, enduring animals, light of foot and very effective for a short dash. They can live upon little, and pick up a subsistence where larger, more carefully trained horses would starve."

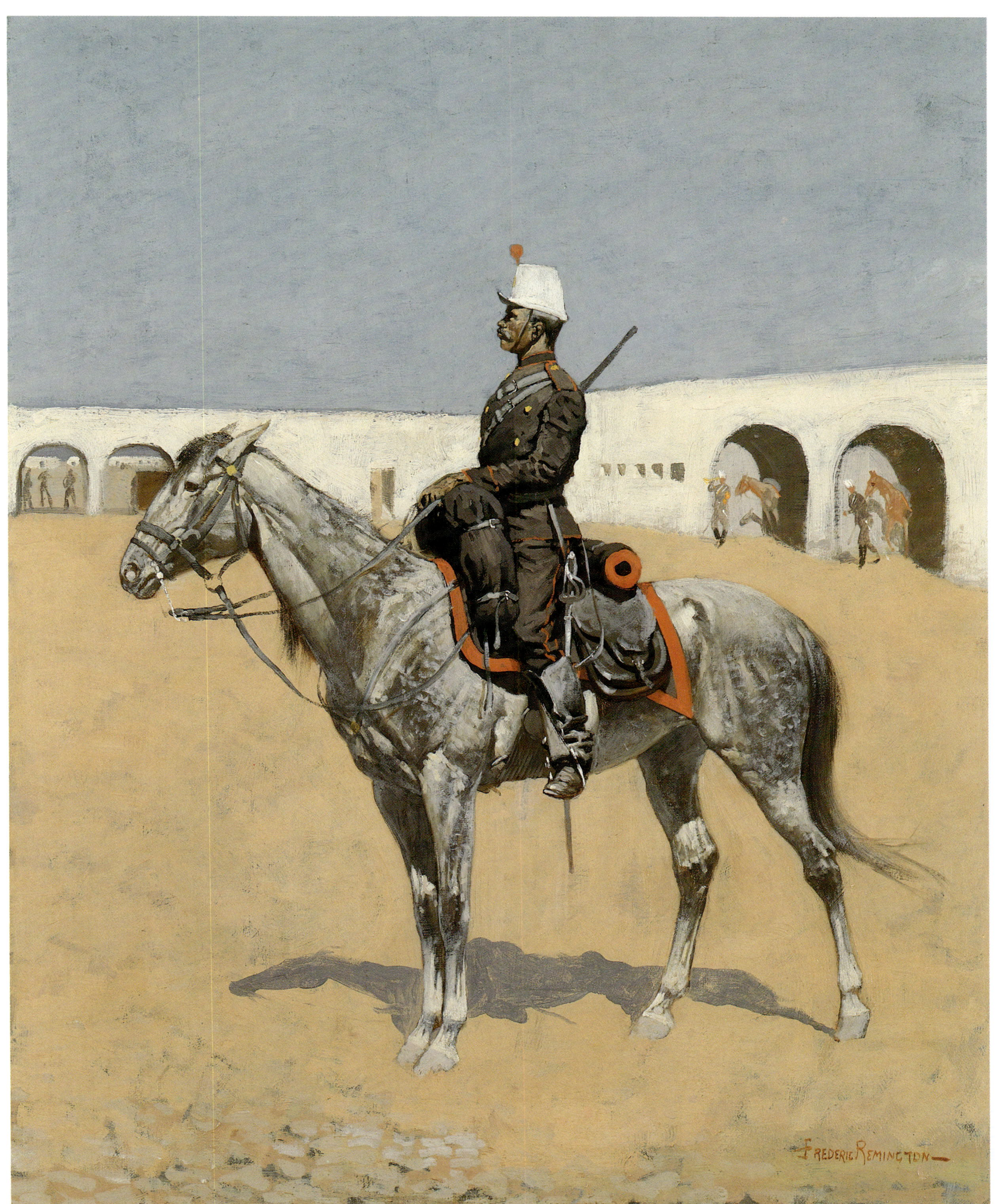
FREDERIC REMINGTON

Cavalry in an Arizona Sandstorm

c. 1889, oil on canvas, 22⅛ x 35¼ inches

When Remington journeyed to Arizona in the summer of 1888 to ride with a U.S. cavalry unit at Fort Grant, he continued his important friendship with Powhatan Henry Clarke, an army lieutenant a year younger than he. Clarke proved to be an invaluable source of information for the rising artist, and their correspondence blossomed until 1893, when the young officer accidentally drowned. The character type that Remington saw in Clarke—a handsome, brash officer whose exploits frequently ran afoul of his superiors—would appear in many of his subsequent works. Clarke contributed to Remington's art in other ways as well. "Say old top when you write me write sort of descriptive like—all that you see and do down there," Remington wrote him in 1887. "While it is stale matter to you it is of great importance to the undersigned—tell me what you do and U.S. soldiers do these days—write any observations you may make or hear relative to Indians or Mexicans—who knows but you might inspire me to make an illustration. . ." Clarke provided many descriptions and impressions to his artist friend back East, as well as articles of equipment and clothing that Remington requested for his burgeoning studio collection in New Rochelle.

While in Arizona with Clarke, Remington experienced firsthand some of the rigors of cavalry life. On June 17, 1888, he participated in a grueling cavalry march from Fort Grant to Fort Thomas and reported to his wife: "The heat was awful and the dust rose in clouds—men get sulky, go into a comatose state—the fine alkalai dust penetrates everything but the canteens. The color of the command was completely lost." His grisaille painting of a cavalry unit caught in a sudden sandstorm appeared in *Harper's Weekly* for September 14, 1889, as an illustration to an article titled "Cavalry in a Sand-Storm." In words that seem to parallel the scene in Remington's painting, an old soldier vividly described a sandstorm he once experienced in Arizona. "All in one moment the whole sky seemed to rush down upon us as if it were a big pepper-box with the lid off, and instantly all was dark as night, and I felt as if forty thousand ants were eating me up at once," he recalled. "You should have seen how the beasts whisked round to get their backs to it, and ducked their heads down! And how the men shut their eyes and pulled their hats down over their faces, and covered their mouths with their hands! But it was no use trying to keep the dust out; it seemed to get inside one's very skin. When it cleared off we all looked as if we'd been bathing in brown sugar, and you might have raked a match on any part of my skin, and it would have lit right away."

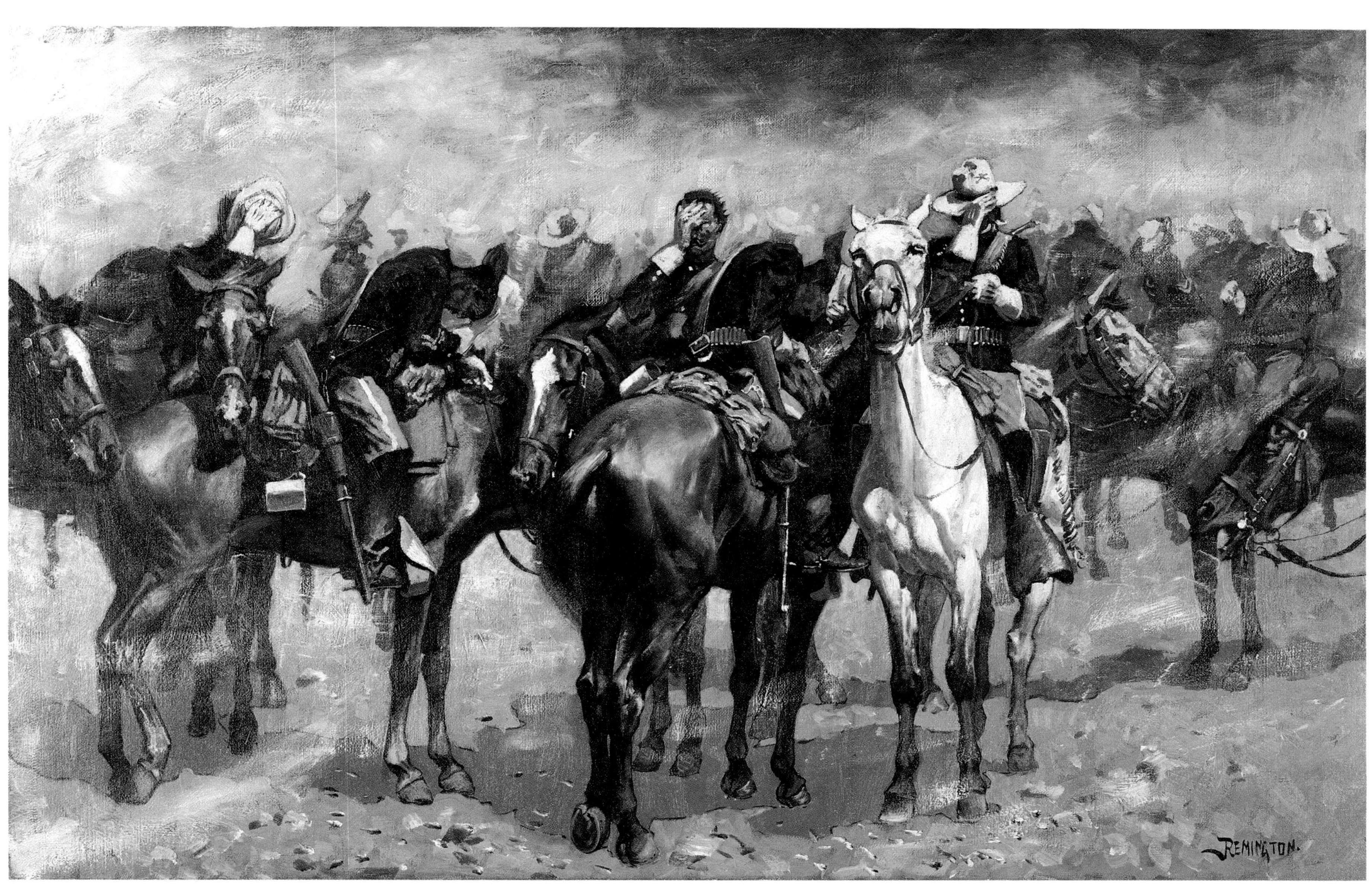
REMINGTON.

Lieutenant S. C. Robertson, Chief of the Crow Scouts

1890, watercolor, opaque white, and graphite on paper, 18⅛ x 13⅛ inches

In October 1890 Remington was invited to travel with an official military commission, headed by Major General Nelson A. Miles, to ascertain the reservation status of the Cheyenne Indians in Montana. The artist, at the time weighing in excess of two hundred pounds, made an amusing sight to the men at Fort Keogh. One, Lieutenant Alvin Sydenham, remarked that his horse "was glad to get rid of him" when he arrived. "Smoothed down over his closely shaven head was a little soft hat rolled up a trifle at the edges," Sydenham recalled. "Tending still more to impress the observer with the idea of rotundity and specific gravity was a brown canvas hunting coat whose generous proportions and many swelling pockets extended laterally, with a gentle downward slope to the front and rear, like the protecting expanse of a brown cotton umbrella." Yet the lieutenant, like the other men in the service, found his guest to be "a fellow you could not fail to like the first time you saw him." For all his seeming awkwardness, Remington proved to be an industrious observer of his surroundings, "his big blue eyes rolling around at everything and into all sorts of queer places." Sydenham also remembered instances when Remington saw something that interested him. "Then I would see him look intently for a moment with his eyes half closed."

Among the things that Remington closely observed at Fort Keogh were the activities of small detachments of Indian scouts, including one led by Lieutenant Samuel C. Robertson. Truly impressed by the Indians in Robertson's Crow Scout Corps from Fort Custer, Remington called them the "best possible" light cavalrymen, second to no one including the white troopers themselves. This watercolor depicts Robertson himself as a figure of regal authority astride a lean, heavily muscled horse. Like the scouts under his command, the lieutenant wears leather leggings in place of high-topped cavalry boots.

The watercolor appeared in the December 27, 1890, issue of *Harper's Weekly*, illustrating Remington's article titled "Indians as Irregular Cavalry." Remington characterized Lieutenant Robertson as "another zealous young man with a fiery purpose to have the best scout corps on the crust of the earth. . . . This is the sort of man who should take the place of the ha'penny politician who has been nurtured in the belief that to plunder the Indians is a natural reward for good service in his district." A few days later, Remington received a letter of thanks from Robertson. Speaking for himself and his fellow officers, Robertson gratefully wrote: "It is not too much to say that I believe your pencil has done more for us than any other single influence I know of."

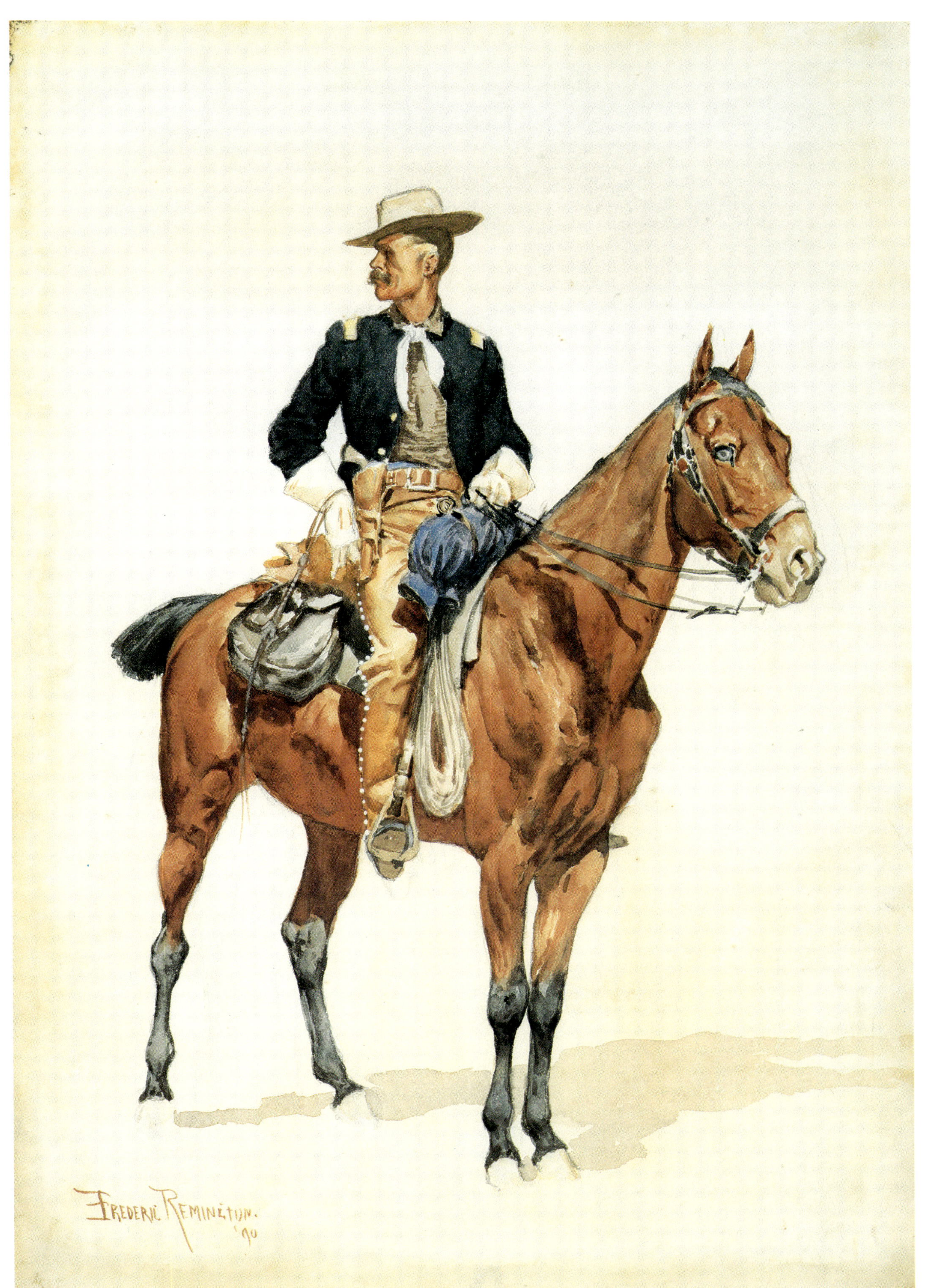
FREDERIC REMINGTON.
'90

A Cavalryman's Breakfast on the Plains

c. 1892, oil on canvas, 22⅛ x 32⅛ inches

Shortly before his article on Indian scouts appeared in a December 1890 *Harper's Weekly*, Remington found himself hurrying back to Sioux country with General Miles' contingent to cover a threatened outbreak of hostilities. On December 15, Indian police at the Standing Rock Agency had murdered the great Sioux chief Sitting Bull. From Miles' headquarters at Rapid City, Remington elected to ride along with Lieutenant Edward Casey's Cheyenne scouts, who were to keep the general and his staff informed of movements by Indian bands to the south. While Remington was with Casey's unit, a tragic action with far-reaching consequences occurred not far away, on Wounded Knee Creek. There, on December 29, the Seventh Cavalry blundered into a massacre of more than 150 Sioux, many of them women and children. General Miles, outraged by the event, immediately convened a court of inquiry, but Remington celebrated the "battle" as a glorious army triumph in an article in *Harper's Weekly*. Unfortunately, his artistic role as the champion of the army made him blind to the darker aspects of the truth.

By the time Remington completed *A Cavalryman's Breakfast on the Plains*, his career was at a high point. He was elected an Associate of the National Academy of Design, a singular honor and a clear indication that he had "arrived" as an artist. Full of confidence concerning his abilities, he continued to refine his skills as a painter. As scholars have shown, Remington's style was influenced by the hard-edged realism of the French military painters, whose works were available to him through reproductions or in the original at museums such as the Metropolitan Museum of Art in New York. As the artist's friend Julian Ralph noted in 1895: "Without imitating any Frenchman, without an inspiration that he consciously owes to France, he yet is French in the stubborn allegiance to truth that he puts in every picture he makes." But at the same time, Remington was following a well-established and typically American strain of direct naturalism. For the group of soldiers in the foreground, the artist actually borrowed an earlier composition of his own, a sketch done during his trip to Arizona and New Mexico in 1888. As the demand for his work steadily increased, he continued to tap the wellspring of his earlier field work for inspiration. *A Cavalryman's Breakfast on the Plains* was included in Remington's first one-man exhibition and auction of nearly one hundred works at the American Art Galleries in January 1893. Practically all of the pieces were sold, and the receipts nearly equalled those of the entire annual show at the National Academy of Design.

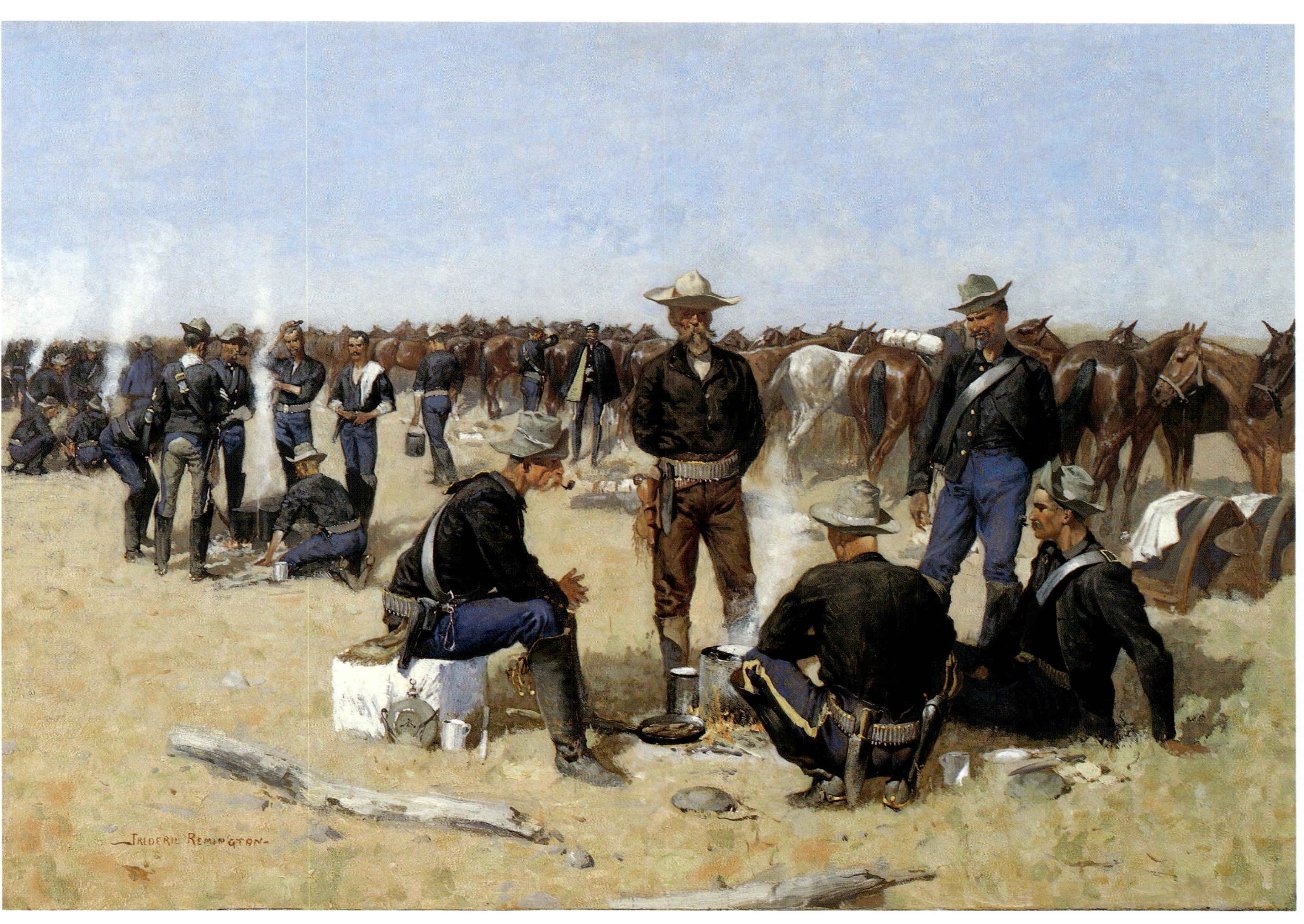
FREDERIC REMINGTON

The Fall of the Cowboy

1895, oil on canvas, 25 x 35⅛ inches

During a trip to Yellowstone Park in the summer of 1893, Remington met Owen Wister, a writer from Philadelphia who was at the beginning of a notable career. The two established an instant friendship; Wister was on assignment for *Harper's* to write a series of articles on "the whole adventure of the West," and Remington was its potential illustrator. In the series of projects that followed, Wister provided the writing and Remington furnished the sketches and plenty of free advice to his less-experienced counterpart. In September or October 1894, Remington wrote: "Say Wister—Go ahead please—make me an article on the evolution of the puncher—the 'passing' as it were. . ." In this and other letters that followed, the artist outlined what he thought the article's contents should be. He described the cowboy's origins in the Southwest as "pure Texan" and his life on the open range as a heroic era "when he literally fought his right of way." Now, according to Remington, the true cowboy was mostly extinct. "Don't mistake the nice young men who amble around wire fences for the 'wild rider of the Plains,'" he warned.

Wister's article, titled "The Evolution of the Cow-puncher," finally appeared, after much rewriting, in the September 1895 issue of *Harper's Monthly*. It was accompanied by a number of illustrations, including *The Fall of the Cowboy*, the painting reproduced here. Beneath a sky with tones of gunmetal gray, two cowboys have halted their horses in a wintry landscape. One of them has dismounted to remove the rails of a gate so they can pass through. The whole scene is infused with the slow rhythms and somber tones of an elegy. "Three things swept [the cowboy] away," Wister wrote, echoing what Remington had told him, "the exhausting of the virgin pastures, the coming of the wire fence, and Mr. Armour of Chicago, who set the price of beef to suit himself." Yet Wister also made a claim of his own; in a flush of romantic illusion, he described the cowboy as an "American descendant of Saxon ancestors," superior to his Hispanic counterpart. Remington was not comfortable with this view and expressed his disapproval long before the article was finally published. "Strikes me there is a good deal of English in the thing—I never saw an English cow-boy—have seen owners," he wrote Wister in February. "You want to credit the Mexican with the inventing [of] the whole business—he was the majority of the 'boys' who first ran the steers to Abilene Kansas."

Remington—like the other great popularizer of the West in this period, Theodore Roosevelt—viewed the cowboy as the last figure of American frontier history: hardy, self-reliant, and tragically doomed to extinction in the wake of civilization's progress. This mythic image was to be immortalized with the publication of Wister's influential novel, *The Virginian*, in 1902.

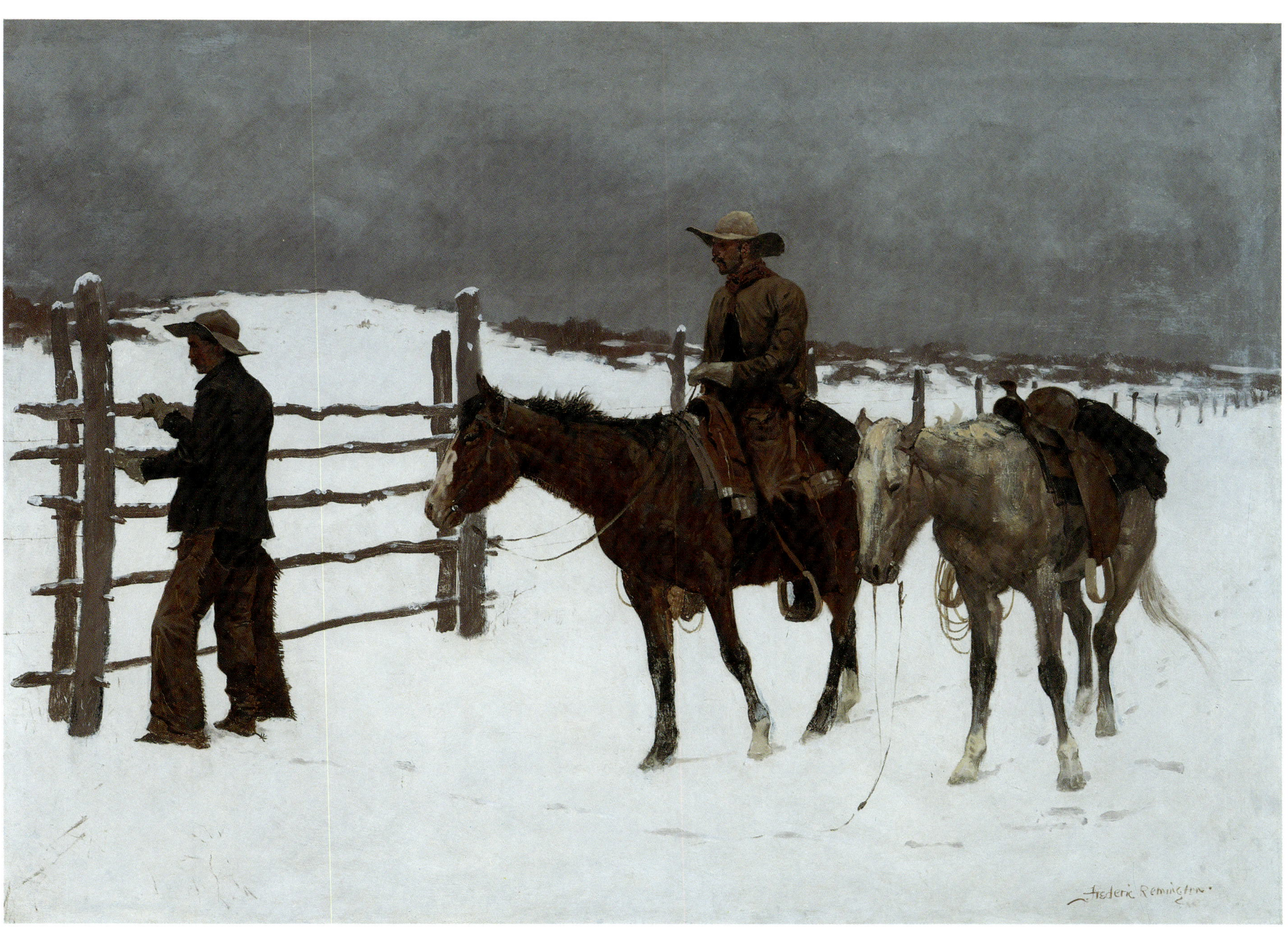
Frederic Remington.

The Bronco Buster

Design copyrighted 1895
Bronze, sand cast #32, 1895, by the Henry-Bonnard Bronze Company, 23½ x 19½ x 12¾ inches

Through the middle months of 1895, Remington was interested in Owen Wister's progress on the cowboy essay for *Harper's* because he was rushing through the process of creating an immortal cowboy of his own. He had discovered the three-dimensional medium of sculpture, and with the advice and encouragement of sculptor Frederic Ruckstull, Remington began modeling a two-foot-high wax depiction of a cowboy on a bucking bronco. "My oils will all get old and watery—that is they will look like *stale molasses* in time—my watercolors will fade—but I am to endure in bronze—even rust does not touch," he excitedly wrote Wister in January 1895. "I am modeling—I find I do well—I am doing a cow boy on a bucking broncho and I am going to rattle down through all the ages." By August the model was completed, and Remington's achievement was nothing short of astounding. With virtually no prior training as a sculptor, he had created one of the most technically accomplished and aesthetically satisfying equestrian subjects in the history of American sculpture.

Remington took his model to a respected foundry, the Henry-Bonnard Bronze Company in New York. There they took a plaster cast of the model, cut the cast into pieces, and made separate molds of baked sand to hold the molten bronze. After the individual pieces had cooled, they were reassembled for final finishing and patination, or coloring. The completed casts were consigned for sale at Tiffany's on Fifth Avenue, and Remington hoped to gain as much profit as notoriety from his new venture.

The work was a great success, and praise came quickly. "The serious fight between man and animal is given with a realism and intensity that come only from profound knowledge," a critic observed in *Harper's Weekly* for October 19, 1895. "Mr. Remington has handled his clay in a masterly way, with great freedom and a certainty of touch, and in a manner to call forth the surprise and admiration not only of his fellow craftsmen, but of sculptors as well." *Century Magazine* for June 1896 published photographs showing the sculpture from four angles to underscore its revolutionary canti-levered composition; Remington's understanding of balance and form had left nearly every American and European sculptor flat-footed. The accompanying article noted the tensile strength of the frozen motion, which "suggests the power of a tightly coiled spring, ready to snap forward." Remington himself was quoted as saying that sculpture "was a great art and satisfying to me, for my whole feeling is for form." William Dean Howells, then regarded by many as the dean of American letters, wrote the artist with words of unbounded praise. "Where is the Broncho Buster to be seen? The picture of the statue took me tremendously. You are such a whaler in every way that it would be no wonder if sculpture turned out to be one of your best holds."

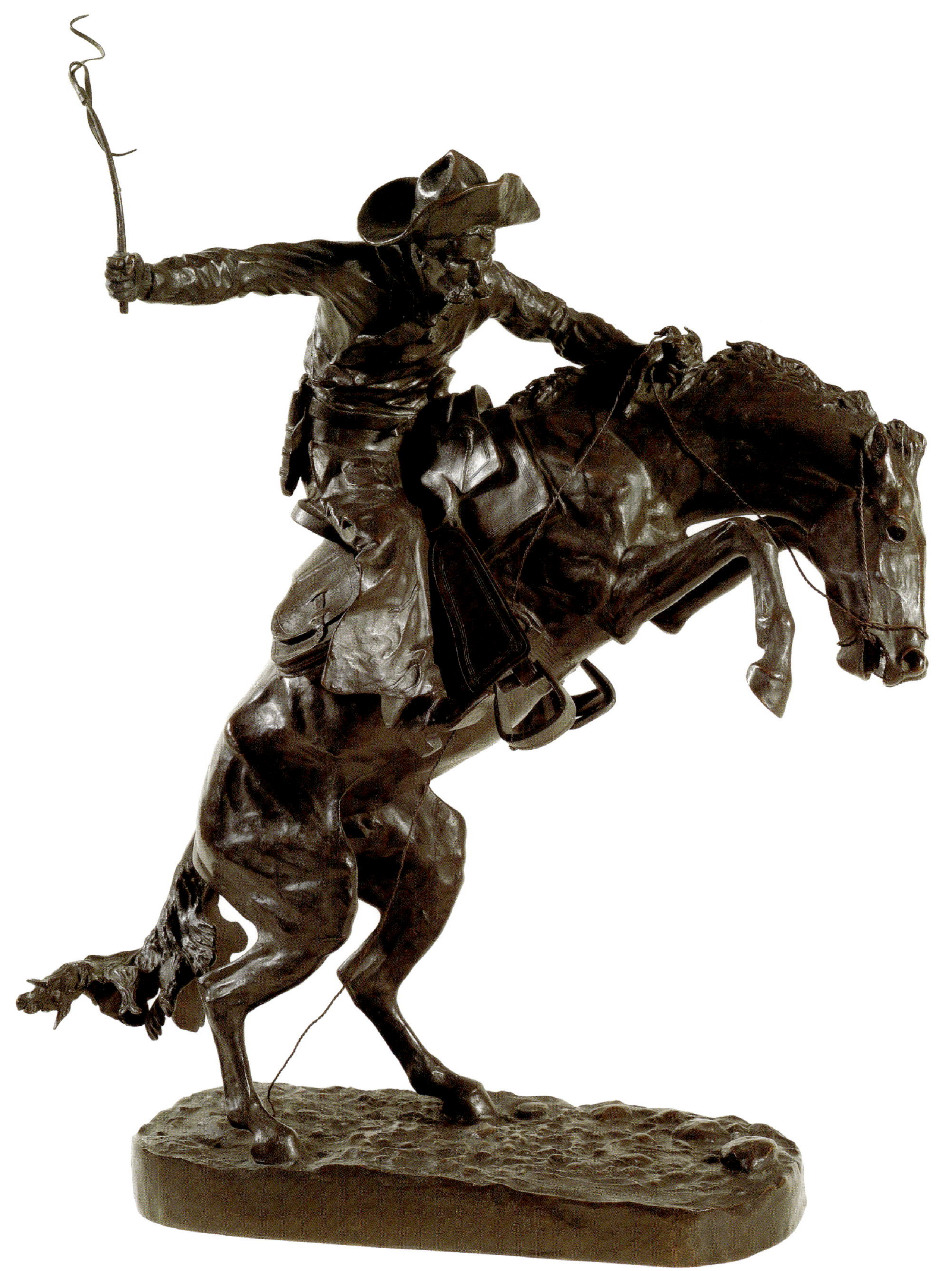

The Wounded Bunkie

Design copyright 1896
Bronze, sand cast letter I, 1899, by the Henry-Bonnard Bronze Company, 20¼ x 32¼ x 13½ inches

For his second subject in bronze, Remington attempted an even more complex essay in arrested motion—two cavalrymen at full gallop, with one soldier falling back wounded and the other reaching over to support him. Here the artist was especially interested in the elements of a moving horse and rider, and the composition seems to defy time and gravity. The sculpture is a high tribute to the skill of the foundrymen at Henry-Bonnard, who worked under Remington's close supervision. Every inch of the richly patinated surface displays the artist's careful attention to detail; all the free elements—reins, canteens, bedrolls, swords, and rifles—had to be cast separately and attached to the finished work.

Soon after *The Wounded Bunkie* appeared, a note in the November 28, 1896, *Harper's Weekly* featured three views of the piece and an explanation of the "rough and ready friendships" among soldiers that the subject's title indicated. "Be the night cold and the position exposed, there is always some one man with whom he will share his blanket or the last drop in his canteen; one companion for whose safety in time of peril he will risk even his own life," it explained. "That man is his 'bunkie.'" The author then marveled at the sense of "free action" the sculpture conveyed, where "the nigh hind leg of one horse and nigh fore leg of the other are contrived to support and balance the whole group in the most natural manner possible."

To develop the seeming realism of his subject, Remington relied on his own observations and the medium of photography. Eadweard Muybridge had published his revolutionary stop-action photographs of humans and animals in motion more than a dozen years earlier, and Remington was among the first artists—and the first sculptor—to carry the new discoveries into his own depictions. He was always quick to point out that he used the camera as a tool, a means to an end. "I've taken lots of photographs of horses myself, and they never give you the feeling of motion," he wrote at one point. "The camera paints what it sees and not what our eyes see." Remington realized he had to exaggerate the motion of a running horse to make it more believable to the viewer. By the time he was beginning to think about modeling sculpture, he had acquired a greater understanding of the forms of art as opposed to those of reality.

Remington spent most of his professional life carefully observing men and horses under a variety of conditions. One of his closest friends, the writer Julian Ralph, emphasized this in an appreciation written for *Harper's Weekly* on July 20, 1895. Ralph acknowledged that "Remington loves the horse, but what not everyone knows is that he said that he would be proud to have carved on his tombstone the simple sentence, 'He knew the horse.'"

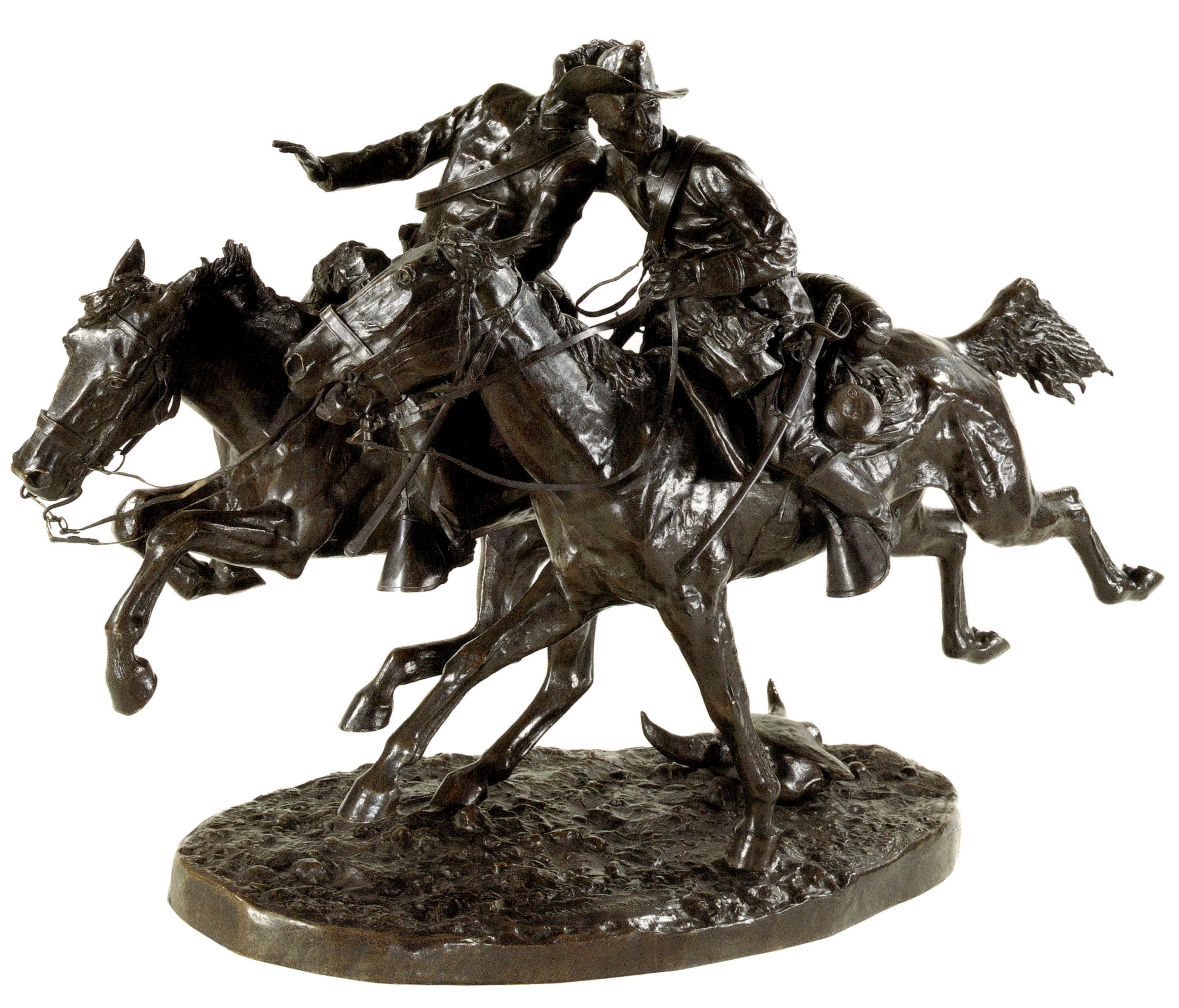

Through the Smoke Sprang the Daring Soldier

1897, oil on canvas, 27¼ x 40 inches

At the same time his artistic career was flourishing, Remington continued to develop his skills as a writer. His first volume of collected stories, titled *Pony Tracks* (1895) and dedicated to "the fellows who rode the ponies that made the tracks," helped establish his stature as a writer. One reviewer called it "a better idea of army life on the western border than all the official records." Drawing on his personal contacts and observations, Remington frequently created his own stories as a means of publishing his illustrations. One example was "A Sergeant of the Orphan Troop," which appeared in the August 1897 *Harper's New Monthly Magazine*.

The story centered on one of the artist's old friends, Sergeant Carter Johnson, who had related the exploits of his career to Remington while the latter accompanied the Tenth Cavalry in Arizona and New Mexico in 1888. Near Fort Robinson, Nebraska, Johnson's unit had fought a number of skirmishes with a band of Northern Cheyenne led by Dull Knife. "It was January; the snow lay deep on the ground, and the cold was knifelike as it thrust at the fingers and toes," Remington wrote of the desperate standoff between the army units and the grimly determined yet outnumbered Indians. "For ten days the troops surrounded the Indians by day, and stood guard in the snow by night, but coming day found the ghostly warriors gone and their rifle-pits empty. They were cut off and slaughtered daily, but the gallant warriors were fighting to their last nerve." The remaining Cheyenne retreated to well-fortified bluffs for a last stand. "Within nine feet of the pits was a rim-rock ledge over which the Indian bullets swept, and here the charge was stopped," Remington wrote. "It now became a duel. Every time a head showed on either side, it drew fire like a flue hole." Suddenly Sergeant Johnson "sprang on the ledge, and like a trill on the piano poured a six-shooter into the entrenchment, and dropped back." He soon found himself in a duel with a warrior named White Antelope, who answered the sergeant volley for volley, until "through the smoke sprang the daring soldier" to deliver the fatal bullets to his adversary.

Remington considered Johnson's bravery the high point of the conflict and immortalized it in the painting, *Through the Smoke Sprang the Daring Soldier*. The point of view is wholly from the army side, with the bedraggled enemy nowhere to be seen. Yet if the painting seems one-sided, the story also recorded Johnson's disgust at a victory won with overwheming odds and grim results. After the final charge, when the air grew clear, "buffalo-robes lay all about, blood spotted everywhere. The dead bodies of thirty-two Cheyennes lay, writhed and twisted on the packed snow, and among them many women and children, cut and furrowed with lead."

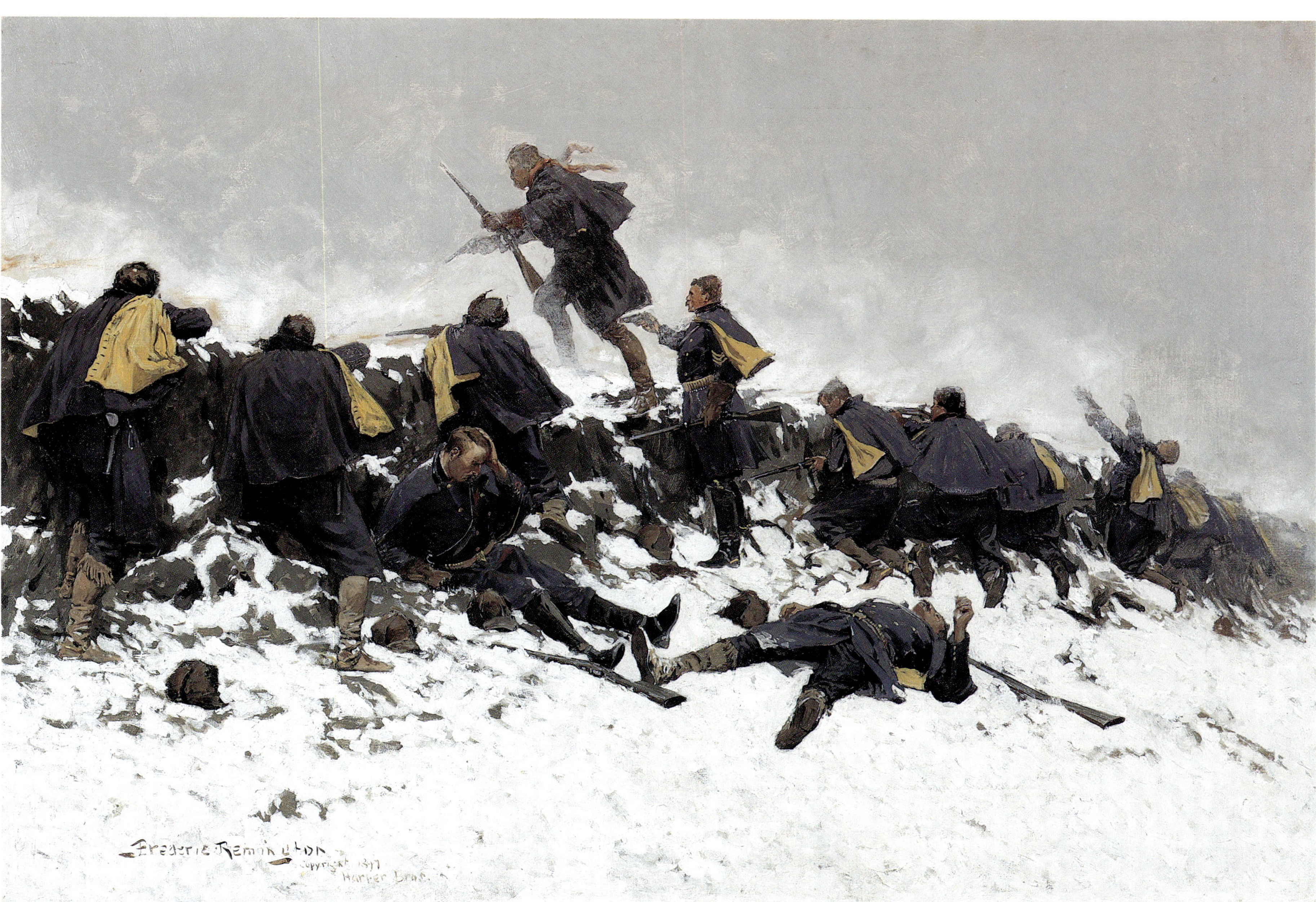
Frederic Remington
Copyright 1897
Harper Bros.

The Wicked Pony

Design copyright 1898
Bronze, sand cast #2, 1898, by the Henry-Bonnard Bronze Company, 22 x 21¼ x 8⅞ inches

Despite its warm reception, sales of *The Wounded Bunkie* proved disappointingly small. Undaunted, Remington returned to a cowboy subject for his third bronze. He wrote Owen Wister in March 1896 and described his "new *mud*—'How the broncho buster got busted'—its going to beat the 'Buster' or be a companion piece." The model, however, spent more than two years in his studio before being cast as *The Wicked Pony*, a work that reversed the triumph of man over animal shown in *The Bronco Buster*.

Ten years earlier, Remington had written an appreciative essay on the wild bronco of the Plains and its actions the first time it was ridden—comparing the experience to being in a railroad accident. "Few Eastern people appreciate the sky-rocket bounds, and grunts, and stiff-legged striking, because the 'bucking' process is entered into with great spirit by the pony but once, and that is when he is first under the saddle-tree." Such a struggle could end in tragedy; Remington supposedly told one admirer of the bronze that he had witnessed the event depicted and that the fallen rider was subsequently killed by the horse's flying hooves. The sculpture, however, shows the moment when the rider has reached out and grasped an ear of the bucking horse, causing its head to drop low to the ground. The composition is quite innovative, unlike any other subject in bronze, leading a critic in the December 17, 1898, issue of *Harper's Weekly* to marvel: "What he has seen in his study of horses and their riders he has seen with such completeness that he can record with accuracy an action which was momentary, or which passed before his eyes like a flash."

Perhaps Remington's desire in 1898 to bring out *The Wicked Pony*, with its less than heroic subject, reflected his own experience as a war correspondent in Cuba that year. The artist had returned from Santiago a changed man, troubled by a new dislike for war and all its manifestations of glory, bravery, and sacrifice. Not surprisingly, the subject of *The Wicked Pony* proved to be a little too depressing for the public, and fewer than ten casts were sold.

In the meantime, sales of the first bronze, *The Bronco Buster*, were continuing apace; by 1900, approximately seventy casts had been made. Remington's spirits received a boost when he found out that a cast of *The Bronco Buster* had been presented to Theodore Roosevelt by his fellow Rough Riders when the unit mustered out of service on Long Island. "I have looked long and hungrily at that bronze, but to have it come to me in this precise way seemed almost too good," Roosevelt wrote the artist. "There could have been no more appropriate gift from such a regiment." Remington was thrilled with the accolade. "The greatest compliment I ever had or ever can have was when the Rough Riders put their brand on my bronze," he told Roosevelt. "After this everything will be mere fuss."

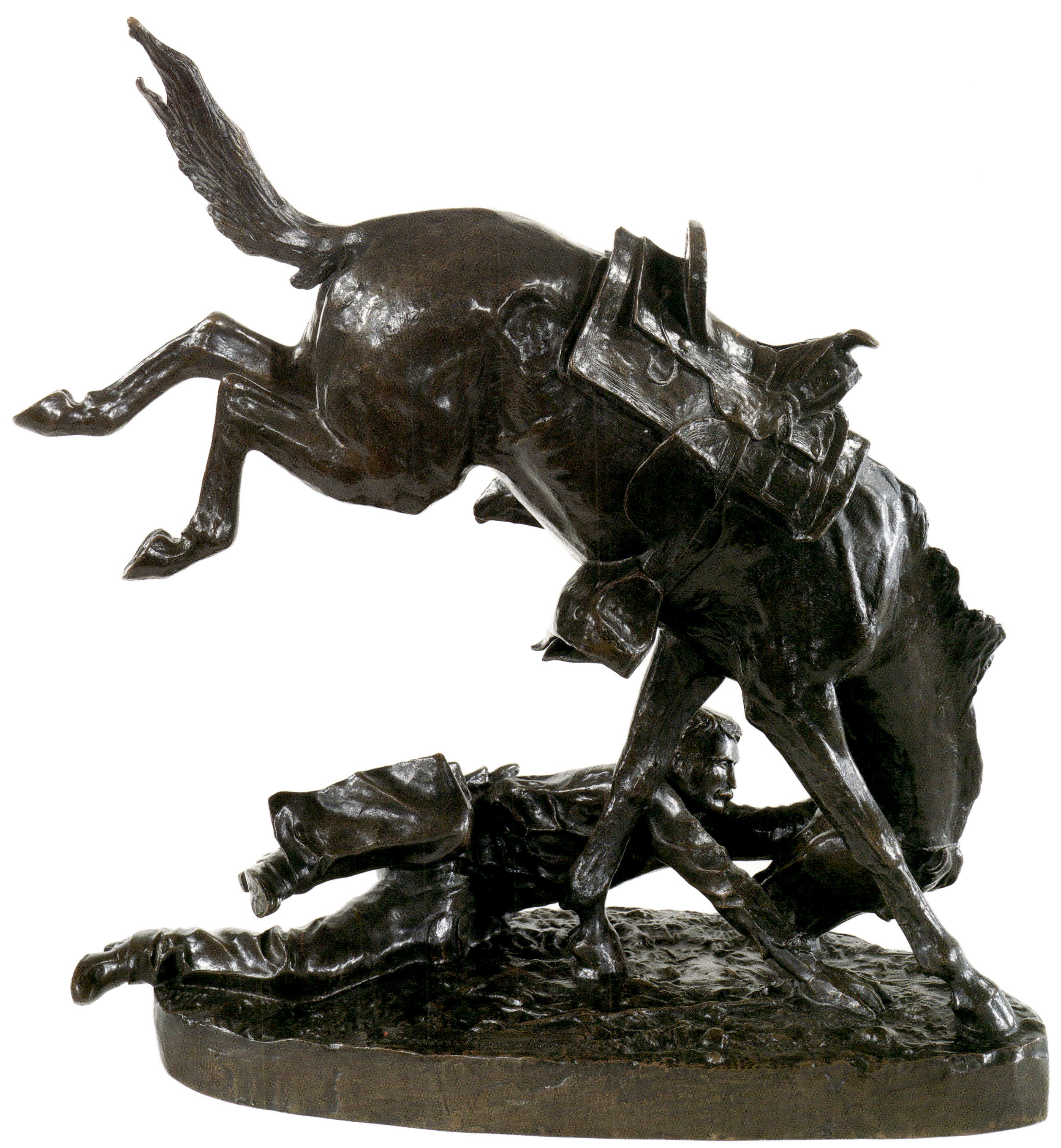

The Scalp

Design copyright 1898 as *The Triumph*
Left: Bronze, sand cast #10, c.1899, by the Henry-Bonnard Bronze Company, 25⅞ x 21 x 7½ inches
Right: Bronze, lost wax cast #6, 1908, by Roman Bronze Works, 25½ x 20⅝ x 10½ inches

Five days after copyrighting *The Wicked Pony*, Remington filed the copyright for his fourth sculpture, *The Triumph*, later known as *The Scalp*. Interestingly, for all the praise the artist's sculpture had received in the press, *The Scalp* was criticized by one academic writer for its "suggestive rather than thorough" modeling and "flat and nerveless" articulation. Such comments seem absurd today, but Remington must have chafed at them. Soon, however, a new alternative to the sand-casting technique became available, enabling the artist to extend his accomplishment in bronze to a new level. By 1900 Remington had learned of the lost-wax casting process and began working with a newly established Brooklyn foundry, Roman Bronze Works, and its energetic proprietor, Riccardo Bertelli, to produce bronze sculptures even more daring in style and technique. This included new versions of two subjects, *The Bronco Buster* and *The Scalp*, done earlier with the sand-cast method.

The two versions of *The Scalp* reproduced here are prime examples of the two casting techniques. The lost-wax cast displays far more detail, including a rougher surface texture that reflects less light. Remington altered the base to a more natural, rock-strewn incline and changed the position of the horse's left rear leg to give more stability to the composition. The deeper modeling and undercutting, evident in such areas as the facial features of the warrior and the adornments of his shield, were made possible by the lost-wax process itself.

This process begins with a gelatin mold taken from the original model to make a negative mold; the gelatin's fluidity allows it to enter deeper recesses and retain finer detail than the fine sand used in the sand-casting technique. Once dry, the gelatin mold is coated on the inside with a layer of wax, then filled with plaster. The gelatin mold is then carefully removed, leaving a wax model of the final bronze that can be altered or adjusted to the artist's content. Remington took full advantage of this fact and expressed his excitement in a *Collier's* article in 1905, around the time he was modeling a new version of *The Scalp*. "Just see what can be done with it—isn't it wonderful! You could work on this for days, changing and rechanging as you like—the only limit is your time and patience." Once he was satisfied with it, the model was encased in an outer mold, fired to melt out the wax layer, and molten bronze poured into the space that remained.

Remington, who became a total convert to this casting technique and established a close working relationship with Bertelli, regularly journeyed to Brooklyn to inspect the plasters or retouch the wax models before they were cast. As a result, bronzes of the same subject made during his lifetime show differences from cast to cast. The artist energetically monitored the production of his bronzes and their eventual sale at Tiffany's, and complained quickly if he felt Bertelli was behind schedule for delivery.

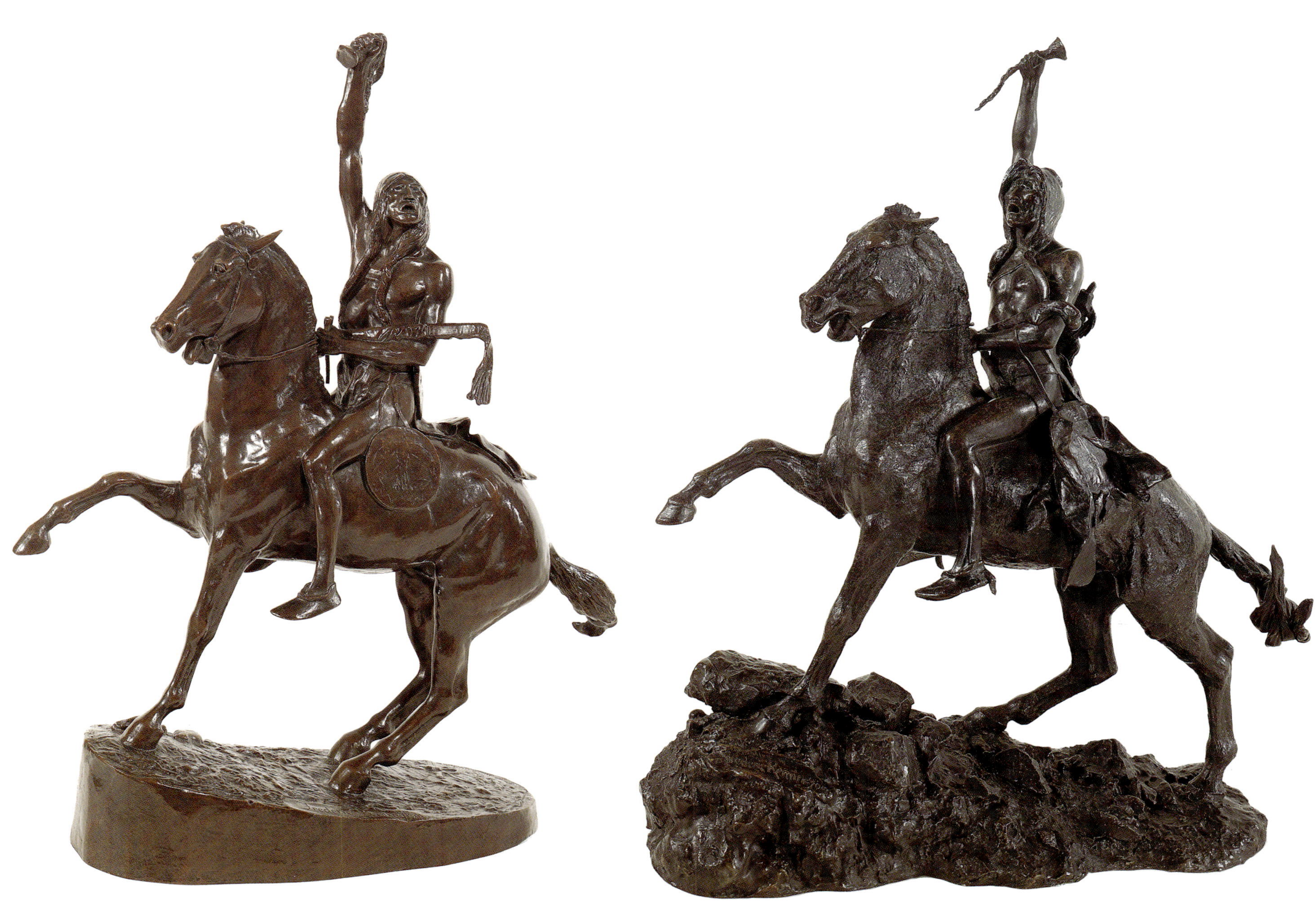

The Cheyenne

Design copyright 1901
Bronze, lost wax cast #20, c.1909, by Roman Bronze Works, 23 1/16 x 7 5/8 x 25 7/8 inches

The lost-wax casting process allowed Remington to push the boundaries of bronze sculpture to their farthest limits, and he soon began to experiment with new subjects that would challenge accepted ideas of mass, gravity, and motion in space. In April 1900, he wrote Owen Wister about a new "mud of an Indian and a pony which is burning the air." This was to be *The Cheyenne*, Remington's sixth bronze in nearly as many years. Riccardo Bertelli was anxious to please Remington as a potential client; consequently, the lifetime casts of the Cheyenne warrior on horseback are among the finest that the foundry ever executed for the artist.

Throughout Remington's brief career as a sculptor, the success of his work depended largely on the partnership that he, as the creative power, maintained with the foundrymen, the artisans capable of carrying his ideas to fruition. Once the bronze had been cast from Remington's wax model, much additional work remained, including grinding, chasing, braising, and coloring the metal surface. Inattention to any of these steps resulted in a bronze cast of inferior quality, and Remington found himself constantly checking the finished work to ensure that it met his own high standards.

In a letter to Bertelli, Remington provided a sketch of *The Cheyenne*, with a vertical axis drawn through the composition's center to show how the buffalo robe support under the horse was to be kept behind the line. "I very much want to preserve the effect of the action which would be ruined by bringing it too far forward," he warned. Bertelli was able to assuage the artist's fears. Seen from the side, *The Cheyenne* is a masterpiece of balance and motion. All four legs of the horse are shown in the tucked position of a full gallop, while elements such as the buffalo robe, the animal's flowing tail, and the decorative tassels of the shield support the feeling of forward progress. In earlier casts, Remington had placed the shield far higher up on the warrior's back; by lowering its position, he could carry the viewer's eye more smoothly from the Indian to the horse, adding to the stability of the composition as a whole.

Remington and the foundry workers also experimented with different surface patinations, or colors, on the casts of *The Cheyenne*. The third cast of the subject, now in the Denver Art Museum, shows variations of green, brown, and yellow, while the cast in the Amon Carter Museum shows the variations of dark green, black, and burnished areas (the latter to achieve a dull coppery color for highlights) that were employed in the majority of the casts. For the most part, the completed bronzes were buffed to a dull finish that would soften the edges of reflected light. While such details might seem picayune, concern for detail produced a work of art of the highest quality.

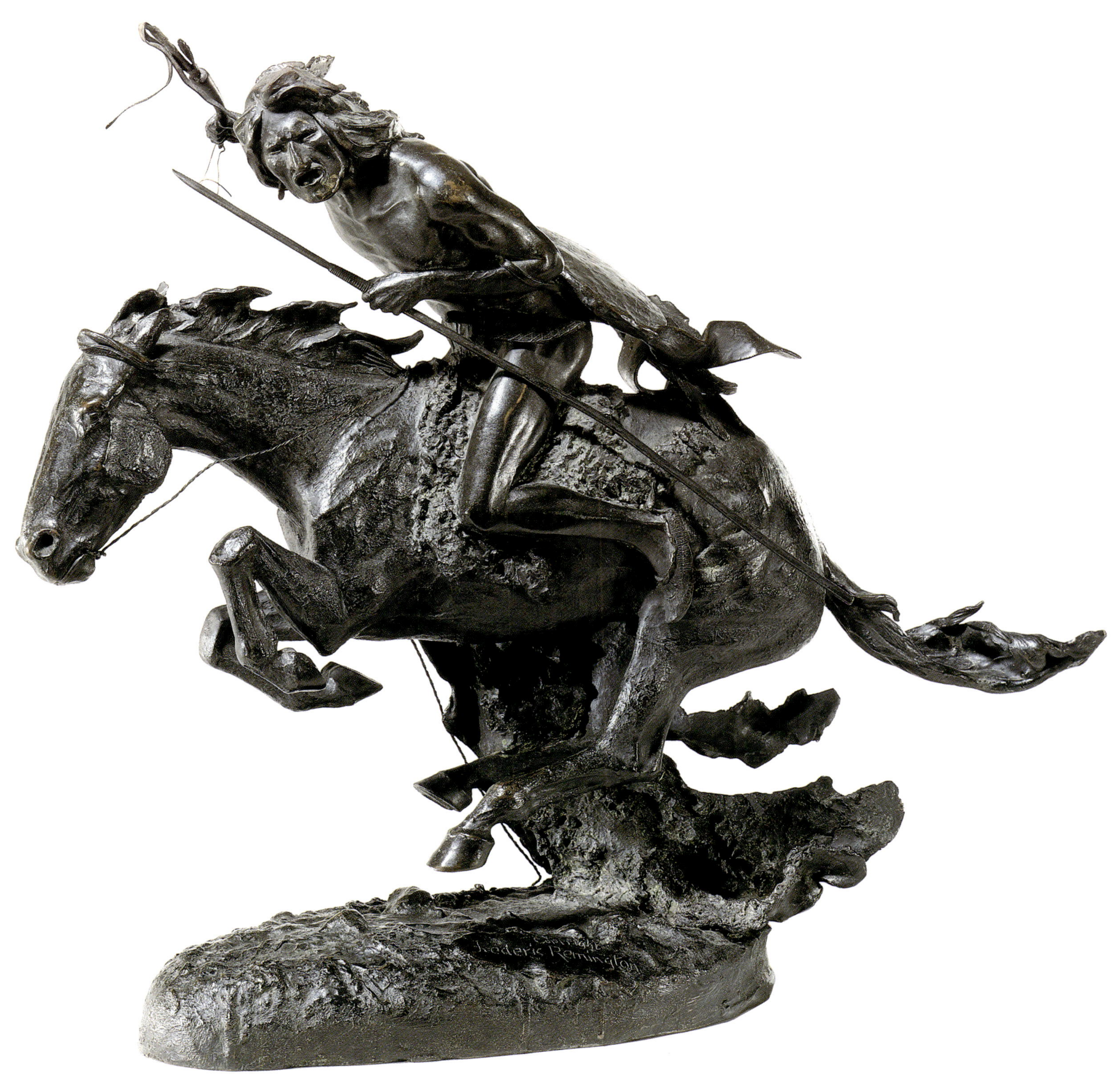

The Old Stage Coach of the Plains

1901, oil on canvas, 40¼ x 27¼ inches

As the new century began, Remington was busier than ever with commissions from several magazines. One of these was to illustrate Emerson Hough's three-part series, "The Settlement of the West: A Study in Transportation," for the *Century Magazine*. Echoing the popular mood of the period, Hough approached his subject with a generalized nostalgia for the "glorious drama" of western settlement. "These days, vivid, adventurous, heroic, will have no counterpart on the earth again," Hough wrote. "There has been close about us for two hundred years the sweeping action of a story keyed higher than any fiction, more unbelievably bold, more incredibly keen in spirit." Attributing much of the story of the West to the development of transportation across the continent, Hough explored all types, from the earliest canoes upon the waters to the far-reaching railroad lines that had bound the West together in more recent times. Remington provided a number of illustrations for Hough's articles; one of these, the evocative depiction of *The Old Stage Coach of the Plains*, appeared as a color plate in the January 1902 issue of *Century Magazine*, accompanying the second installment of Hough's story.

"The pony express was a wonderful thing in its way, and some of the old-time stage lines which first began to run out into the West were hardly less than wonderful," Hough wrote. In describing the two-thousand-mile-long stage run from Atchison, Kansas, to Helena, Montana—which took more than twenty-two days over sometimes very difficult terrain—he related an early account of the route's dangers during a Sioux uprising. The need for constant vigilance against possible attack seems to be the general subject of Remington's interpretation, which shows a stagecoach traveling by moonlight through a nocturnal landscape; atop the coach and silhouetted against the starlit sky is a figure with a rifle. Like Hough, Remington was evoking a sense of nostalgia for a mythic West that had entered the popular imagination.

The whole work is loosely painted with shadowy tones of brown, green, and blue that occasionally form glimmering highlights. At the time, Remington was developing a much greater interest in color for its own sake, especially its expressive possibilities. In 1899, at the Union League Club, he viewed an influential exhibition featuring the work of Charles Rollo Peters, a California tonalist painter who specialized in nocturnal scenes. Scholars have shown that Peters' example inspired Remington to experiment with a more narrow and muted color range in some of his paintings, including *The Old Stage Coach of the Plains*. Gradually, the artist began to eliminate detail from such works in favor of a general mood and atmosphere.

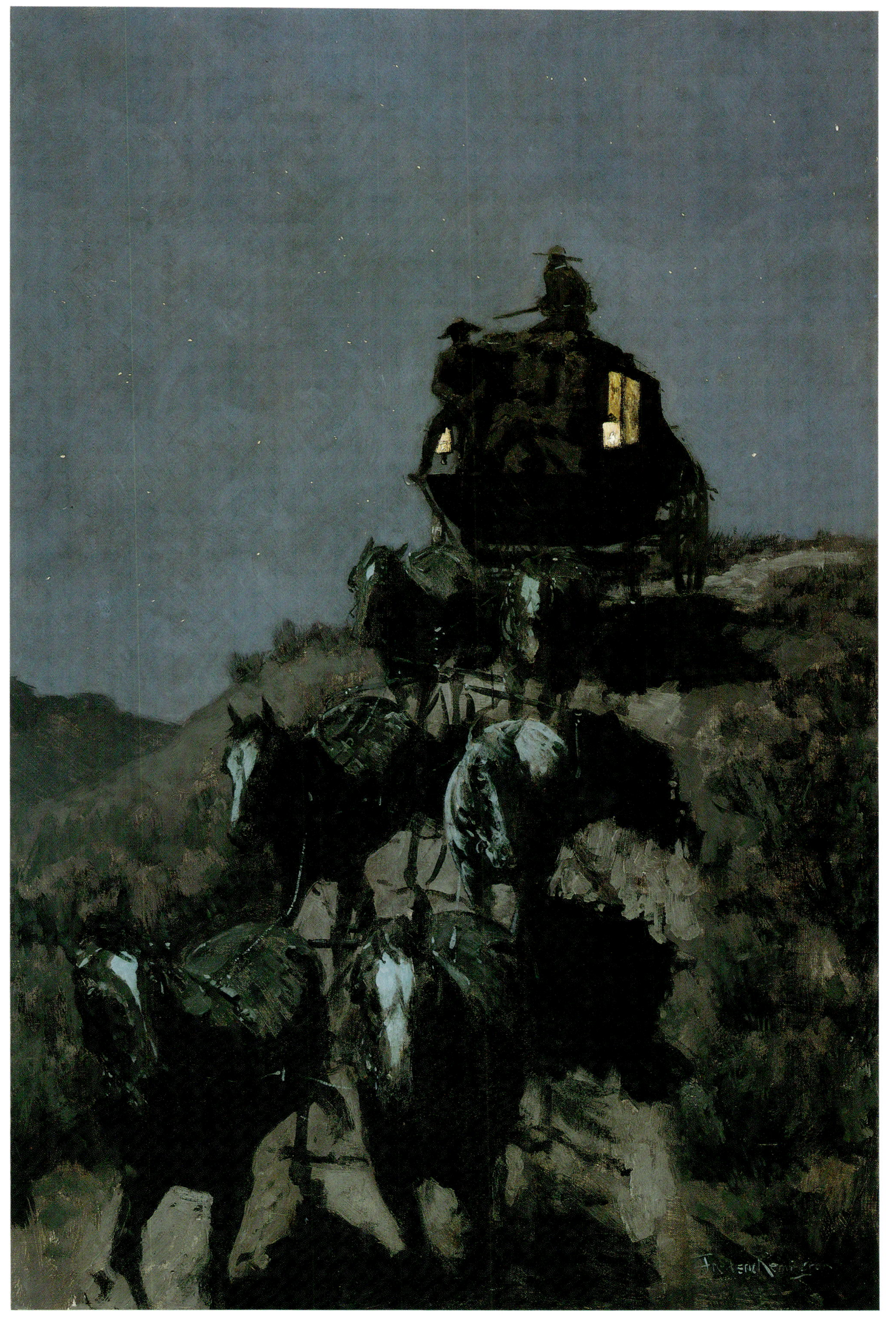

Infantry Soldier

1901, pastel and graphite on paper, 29 x 15⅞ inches

By 1901 Remington's long association with the Harper publishing house was all but over. In its place, *Collier's* magazine, with a circulation of close to a quarter of a million, became the artist's principal outlet. *Collier's* was a pictorial magazine, utilizing the most advanced color printing, and Remington's work was frequently displayed by itself, as a double-page spread or cover. The magazine also reprinted some of his paintings in picture books and made individual color reproductions available to the general public at affordable prices. All of this activity helped Remington's vivid images of the American West become absorbed into the mainstream of popular culture.

In early 1902 *Collier's* published one of the most popular compendiums of Remington's work, a portfolio of more than sixty illustrations in black and white titled *Done in the Open*. Reproduced on the cover was the artist's convincing pastel study, *Infantry Soldier*. The previous year, as his interest in color burgeoned, Remington had attempted the medium of pastel in order to create more vibrant effects in his drawings. He produced a number of works, including this example, that showed an astonishing mastery of the technique in so short a time. The deep blue hues of the infantryman's shirt and the earthy yellow tones of his pants are skillfully blended to suggest shadows and folds. The overall effect is a painterly one, with the rich colors blended into a loose yet convincing harmony.

Remington's association with *Collier's* seemed to culminate with the March 18, 1905, issue of the magazine, which was devoted entirely to his work. He was also cajoled into furnishing "A Few Words from Mr. Remington" for the readers. The artist related a formative incident that had occurred during his first visit to the West in 1881, when he met an old wagon freighter who told him stories of the early West and lamented its loss in the face of progress. "There he was, my friend of the open, sleeping on a blanket on the ground (it snowed that night), eating his own villainies out of his frying-pan, wearing a cotton shirt open at the throat, and hunting his horses in the bleak hills before daylight; and all for enough money to mend harness and buy wagon grease," Remington wrote. "He had his point of view and he made a new one for me. . . . I knew the railroad was coming—I saw men already swarming into the land. . . . I knew the wild riders and the vacant land were about to vanish forever, and the more I considered the subject the bigger the Forever loomed. Without knowing exactly how to do it, I began to try to record some facts around me, and the more I looked the more the panorama unfolded." Remington told his readers to be patient with his desire to create a mythic West of the past. "Besides, artists must follow their own inclinations unreservedly," he wrote. "It's more a matter of heart than head, with nothing perfunctory about it. I saw the living, breathing end of three American centuries of smoke and dust and sweat, and I now see quite another thing where it all took place, but it does not appeal to me."

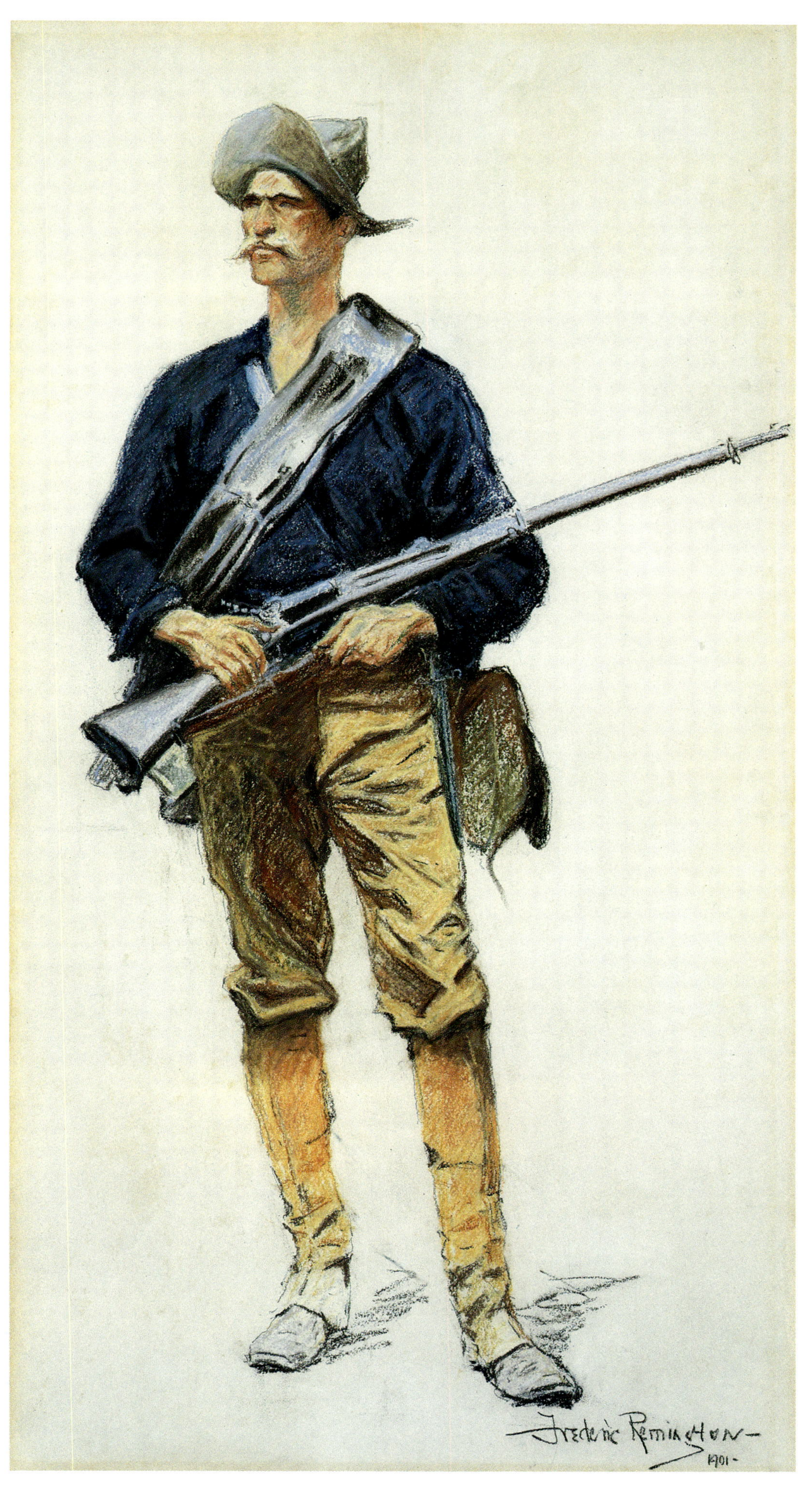
Frederic Remington
1901

The Cowboy

1902, oil on canvas, 40¼ x 27⅛ inches

"No longer strange, and becoming conventional, the cow-boy is merely trying to get mountain-bred ponies to go where he wants them to go," noted the author of the brief text that accompanied Remington's depiction of a cowboy galloping his horse down a steep embankment. *The Cowboy* was one of a series of four paintings reproduced in the October 1902 *Scribner's Magazine* under the title, "Western Types"; the other subjects were *The Scout*, *The Half-Breed*, and *The Cossack Post (Cavalryman)*. The paintings were also offered as individual prints and proved to be very popular with the public. Like the pastel of the *Infantry Soldier*, this painting shows the artist's new awareness of color. Harmonious tones of dusty yellow, light blue, and pale lavender in the landscape that surrounds the charging rider offer an effective contrast to the central figure.

The story is told that John Howard, a boyhood friend of Remington's, greatly admired the painting in the artist's studio and asked its price. Although Remington quoted a price far higher than anticipated, Howard reluctantly agreed to write a check for the amount. Months passed without the check clearing the bank, and Howard found himself having to remind Remington on numerous occasions about their transaction. One evening, as the two men were sitting together after dinner, the artist used a piece of paper to light their cigars. Afterwards, Remington told Howard that the piece of paper was the check and the sale of the painting was at last concluded.

The rise of the cowboy as the romantic hero of the American West began shortly after the Civil War, and many writers and artists, including Remington, played a part in its subsequent development. One of the cowboy's most effective supporters was Theodore Roosevelt, who authored a series of articles describing his experiences as a ranchman in the Dakota Territory. These first appeared, with illustrations by Remington, in *Century Magazine* in 1888–89. Roosevelt viewed cowboys as the final players in the vivid drama of the American frontier, "as hardy and self-reliant as any men who ever breathed," and in describing them, he helped invent that hero-type for future generations. "Peril and hardship, and years of long toil broken by weeks of brutal dissipation, draw haggard lines across their eager faces, but never dim their reckless eyes nor break their bearing of defiant self-confidence," he wrote. "They do not walk well, partly because they rarely do any work out of the saddle, partly because their *chaperajos* or leather overalls hamper them when on the ground; but their appearance is striking for all that, and picturesque too, with their jingling spurs, the big revolvers stuck in their belts, and bright silk hand-kerchiefs knotted loosely round their necks over the open collars of their flannel shirts." He praised the cowboy's strength of character, which included a "frank and simple" approach to life, a "whole-souled hospitality" to others, and an air of "grave courtesy" to outsiders. By the time Owen Wister published his novel *The Virginian* in 1902, such traits were embedded in the role of the central character, and it should not be surprising that Wister dedicated his book to Roosevelt.

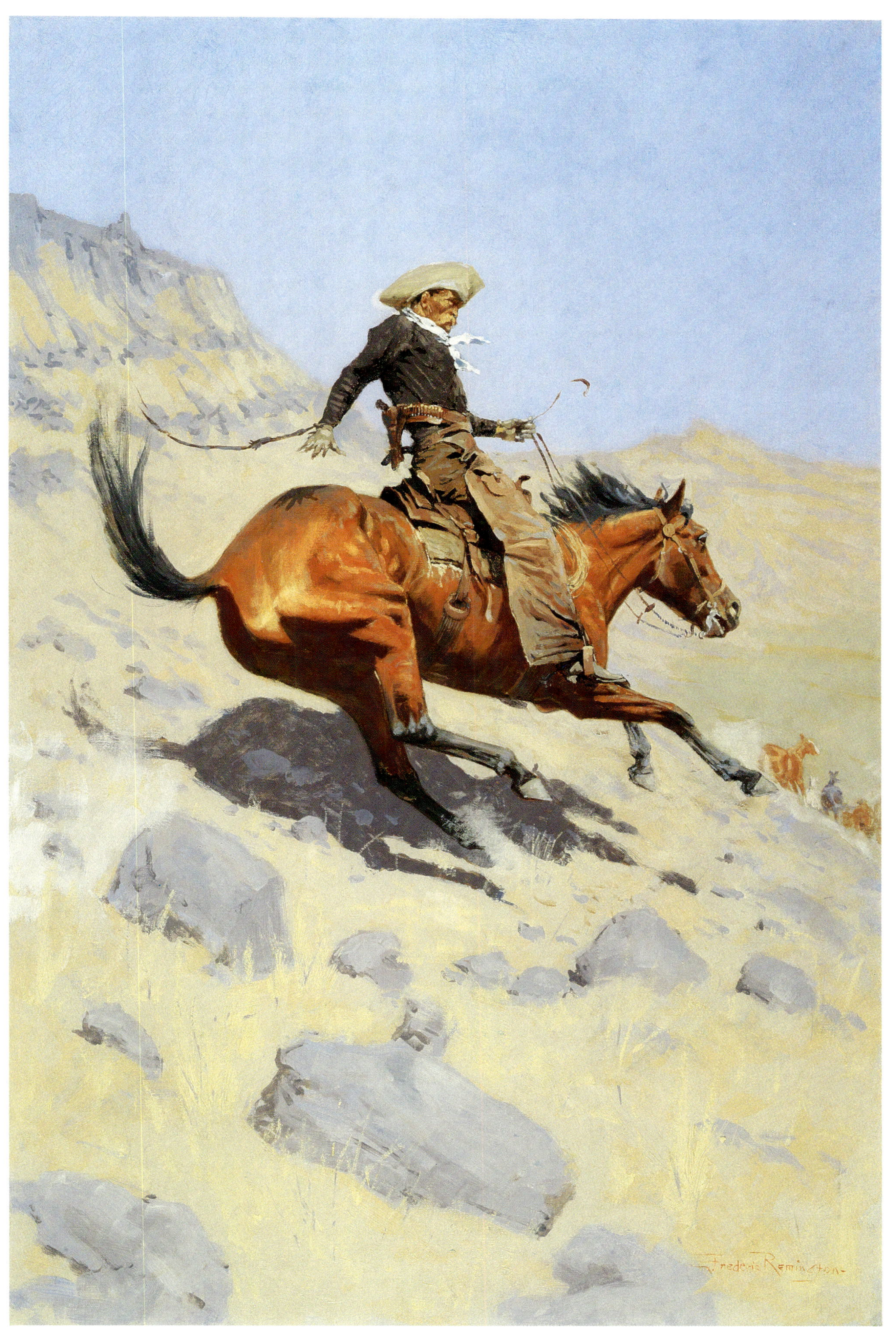
Frederic Remington

A Reconnaissance

1902, oil on canvas, 27¼ x 40⅛ inches

In the last decade of his life Remington worked diligently to develop his painting technique beyond the limits of his earlier work as an illustrator. Although his fame as one of the most accomplished artists of the American West seemed to be assured, Remington continued to find fault with what he perceived as his limitations in painting light and color. In 1905 he had exhibited a number of paintings, including *A Reconnaissance by Moonlight*, at the Noé Art Galleries in New York; the reviews were generally good, but he continued to feel inadequate technically. Despite Remington's own reservations, however, *A Reconnaissance* conveys a unified sense of light and shadow in shifting tones of blue, green, and brown.

In December 1905, when Charles Shepard Chapman was a young artist at the beginning of his career, he visited Remington at Endion, his home and studio in New Rochelle. Chapman recalled Remington, on a walk through the woods behind the house, venting his frustration at not being able to adequately paint the effects of light, particularly at night, on the surface of the snow that blanketed the landscape. Seated before a fire in Remington's studio, the two men continued their conversations about the problems of painting. To Chapman's astonishment, Remington retrieved a group of beautiful landscape sketches in oil and began to criticize them one at a time before casting them into the fire. Billows of smoke from the smothering fire caused Mrs. Remington to appear and frantically admonish her husband to stop, and the half-burned sketches were dropped out a studio window into the wet snow. Remington subsequently said to Chapman: "Every place I go I'm the great Fred Remington, but all my life I've planned what I would paint when I had money enough and for ten years I've been trying to get color in my things and I still don't get it. Why why why can't I get it. The only reason I can find is that I've worked too long in black and white. I know fine color when I see it but I just don't get it and it's maddening. I'm going to if I only live long enough."

Remington's self-criticism seems unduly harsh today, but at the time he yearned for the art establishment to accept him fully as a professional painter. His burgeoning friendships with other artists also turned him more sharply towards the problems of painting for its own sake. In 1900 he acquired a small island on the Saint Lawrence River, where he built a summer home and studio that he named Ingleneuk, and began to spend long hours observing natural light effects, attempting to capture them in countless studies and sketches. He noted his progress in the pages of his personal diary as he struggled with the effects of color in the "wonderful moonlight nights" of the northern woods: "It has not yet been painted but I think I am getting nearer all the time."

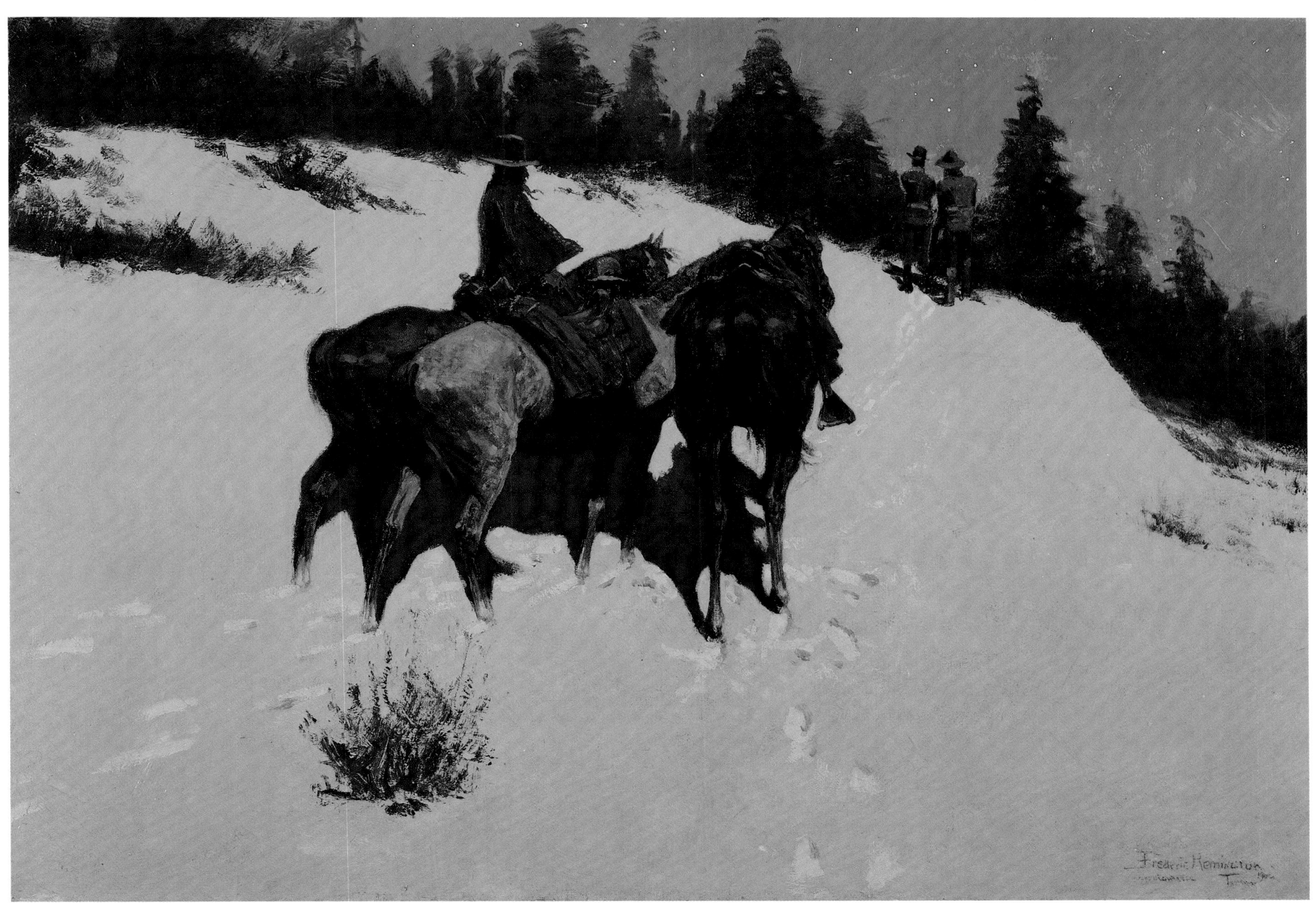
Frederic Remington

His First Lesson

1903, oil on canvas, 27¼ x 40 inches

In September 1903, Remington entered an agreement with *Collier's* to have the magazine reproduce at least one painting per month in full color, without any editorial control or connection to an accompanying text. The contract was to last four years and the artist to receive one thousand dollars per painting, for a minimum of twelve thousand dollars per year. The magazine in turn could issue prints of the paintings it selected for publication. The income was significant, but the arrangement's primary appeal for Remington was that it treated his work as more than mere illustration. During the summer he had written a friend from the Ingleneuk studio that he was "working like hell on stuff which I cannot neglect"—his large paintings for *Collier's*. The first, for the September 26, 1903, issue, was *His First Lesson*, a deftly painted scene derived from the artist's trip to an American-owned ranch in Chihuahua, Mexico, nearly ten years earlier.

Beginning in December 1893, Remington had described life at the ranch in a series of articles for *Harper's Monthly*. The "great straggling square of mud walls" included adobe corrals and outbuildings staffed by American cowpunchers and Mexican vaqueros. "I sat on a mud-bank and worked away at a sketch of the yellow sunlit walls of the mud-ranch, with the great plain running away like the ocean into a violet streak under the blue line of the Peña Blanca," Remington wrote. Those colors dominate *His First Lesson*, in which two cowhands make ready to ride a wary horse whose right rear leg has been tied up with a rope attached to its neck. The cowboys seem to fit Remington's description of the Texas foremen at the ranch, each of whom wore "heavy *chaparras*, a slouch hat, and a white 'biled' shirt." Their duties, according to the artist, comprised "anything and everything," including breaking recalcitrant horses that no one else could ride.

In the painting, Remington's brushwork is more relaxed and soft-edged than in previous works, reflecting his increasing attention to the French-influenced impressionist style. This is particularly evident in the vibrant reflections of color on the stiffened horse and in the dappled brushwork of the cool violet shadows. The sunlit portions of the foreground are small islands of color, in which warm hues of burnt orange and mustard yellow are set against small patches of green that the artist described as "burning bright like opals." One of Remington's subtle skills as an artist can be seen in the way that he has closed one of the windows in the adobe wall in the background; this relieves the visual monotony of a row of dark squares at a point that allows the viewer to focus on the central figure of the painting, the wild-eyed horse.

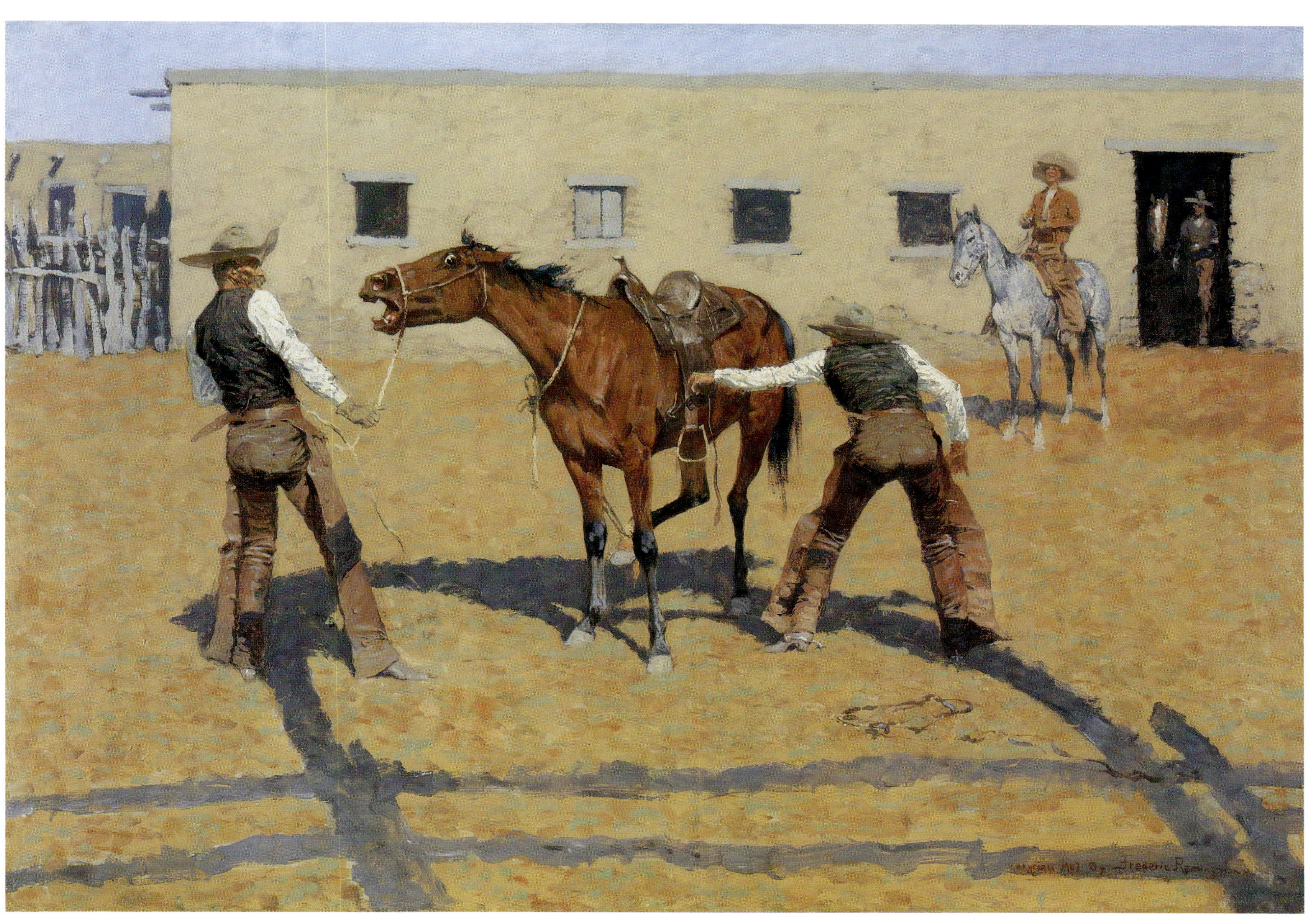

Pony Tracks in the Buffalo Trails

1904, oil on canvas, 30⅛ x 51⅛ inches

In order to satisfy his contract with *Collier's* for at least one major painting every month, Remington reviewed his past experiences for new subjects. *Pony Tracks in the Buffalo Trails*, reproduced as a double-page color spread in the issue for October 8, 1904, seems to have been loosely based on the artist's sojourn in the Sioux country fourteen years earlier, when he accompanied Lieutenant Edward W. Casey's unit of Cheyenne scouts and horse soldiers. Remington wrote several articles about his experiences "in the tangled masses of the famous Bad Lands," where "the painter's whole palette is in one bluff." In the painting reproduced here, four scouts, one of them dismounted, follow a trail looking for signs, while an officer leads a file of cavalry stretching back into the distance.

During this 1890 trip, Remington came the closest to actual conflict. Not long after he left Lieutenant Casey's camp for the Pine Ridge Indian Agency, twenty-five miles distant, in the company of two Indian scouts, a white interpreter, and a teamster and wagon, their party encountered a number of hostile Sioux warriors. A tense conversation ensued between Red Bear, one of the scouts, and a group of the Sioux. The interpreter, who had just relinquished his tobacco pouch to a Sioux warrior, suddenly signaled to Remington that one of the Indians had slipped up behind him. "Turning, I advanced on him quickly (I wanted to be as near as possible, not being armed), and holding out my hand, said 'How colah?' the artist recalled. "He did not like to take it, but he did, and I was saved the trouble of further action." Remington's party quickly decided to turn their wagon around and start back to the camp. Fortunately, they soon encountered five "fully armed, well-mounted cowboys" who sensed the danger and joined the retreat, thus increasing the odds for a successful defense. "We deployed the flanks of the wagon so that the team horses might not be shot, which would have stopped the whole outfit, and we did ten miles at a record-breaking gallop," Remington wrote. "We struck the scout camp in a blaze of excitement. The Cheyennes were in war-paint, and the ponies' tails were tied up and full of feathers."

The narrow escape had an unnerving effect on the artist, and he never forgot it. Paintings like *Pony Tracks in the Buffalo Trails* celebrate the everyday gallantry and courage of the frontier regulars and the professional officers who led them. The artist was deeply grieved to learn, soon after he returned to the East, that Lieutenant Casey was dead, shot from behind during an Indian parley. For Remington, the sacrifices of such men were not to be in vain.

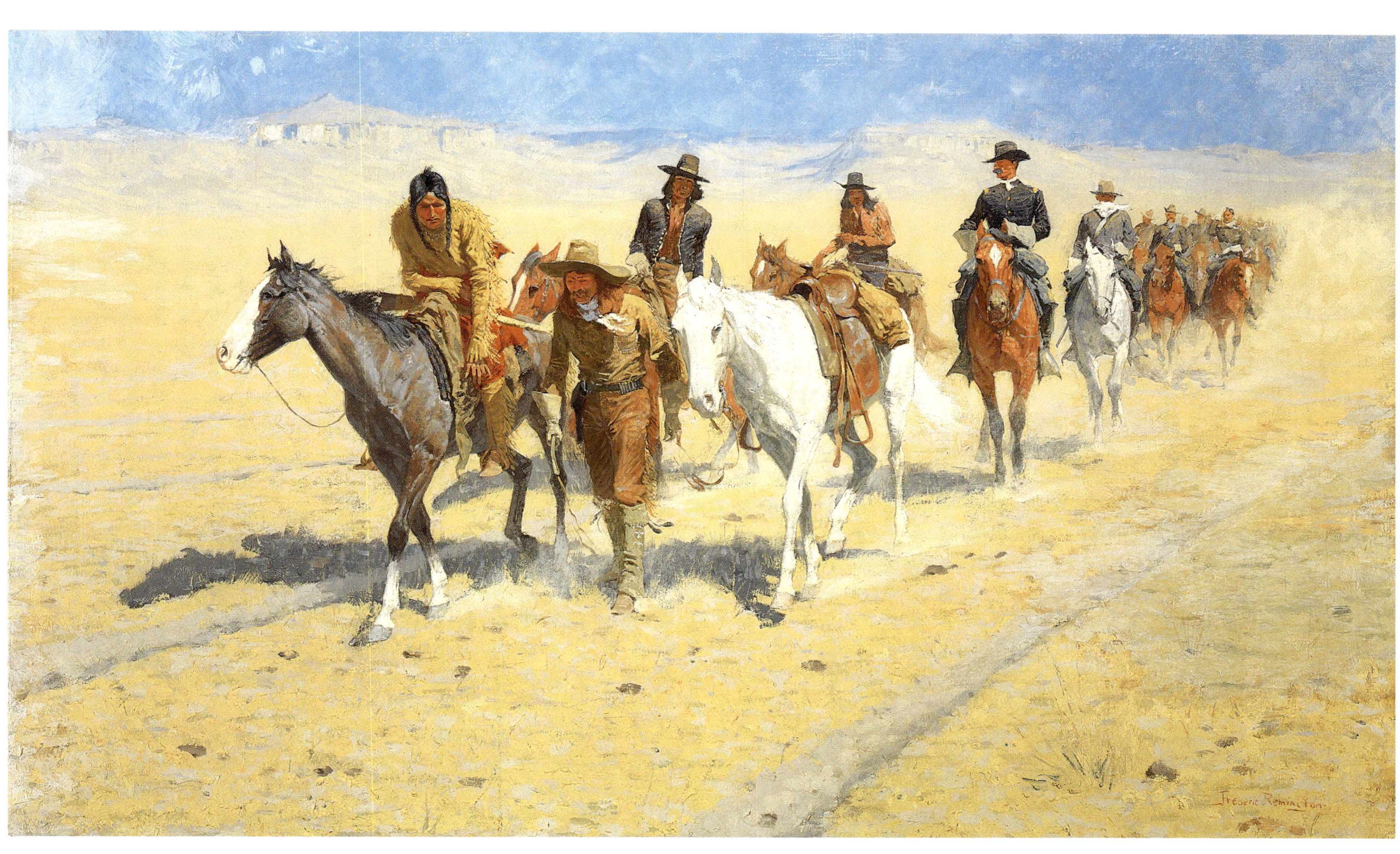

Ridden Down

1905, oil on canvas, 30¼ x 51¼ inches

In September 1905 Remington took a nostalgic sketching trip back to the South Dakota Badlands where he had experienced his adventures with the Cheyenne scouts fifteen years before. Soon after his return to New Rochelle, *Cosmopolitan* magazine began publishing serial installments of one of the artist's most successful novels, *The Way of an Indian*. The life story of a Cheyenne, told from his point of view, it chronicles the life and death of a people. While undergoing a medicine ordeal, the young Cheyenne finds his spiritual emblem in a small brown bat and takes the name Ho-to-kee-mat-sin, or The Bat. He develops into a skilled warrior who triumphs over his enemies, including white traders and trappers, then rises to a chieftain's rank and takes the name Fire Eater. He becomes increasingly powerless as his tribe falls before the encroachments of white settlement, and when the U.S. Cavalry attacks their village at night, Fire Eater and his warriors are decisively defeated. The few survivors, including the aging chief, escape to the mountains, but his people have been destroyed, his youngest son killed, and his medicine bundle with all its spiritual strength has been lost. The novel ends with the despairing Fire Eater sitting alone, "waiting for the evil spirits which lurked out among the pine trees, to come and take him. He wanted to go to the spirit-land where the Cheyennes of his home and youth were at peace in the warm valleys, talking and eating."

Although *The Way of an Indian* did not become a best-seller, the press responded warmly, praising it as a "sympathetic and deeply probing" description of the Indian experience. "It may be true no white man ever understood an Indian," Theodore Roosevelt wrote the artist from the White House, "but at any rate you convey the impression of understanding him!"

The themes in Remington's novel have their visual counterpart in *Ridden Down*, completed the same year. Here a lone warrior, stripped for battle and covered with protective green "medicine" paint, stands on the edge of a bluff next to his gasping, sweat-lathered horse, which has been ridden to exhaustion. A badlands landscape stretches all around them like an ocean of shimmering yellow, and an indistinct band of Indians on horseback gallops toward them from the desert flats below. Like Fire Eater in Remington's novel, this warrior stoically awaits his inevitable fate, but this time he retains his medicine and prepares to use it to the last. The story told by the painting is simple, yet powerful. "Big art is the process of elimination," Remington was quoted as saying in an *Outing* magazine interview in March 1903. "Cut down and out—do your hardest work outside the picture, and let your audience take away something to think about—to imagine."

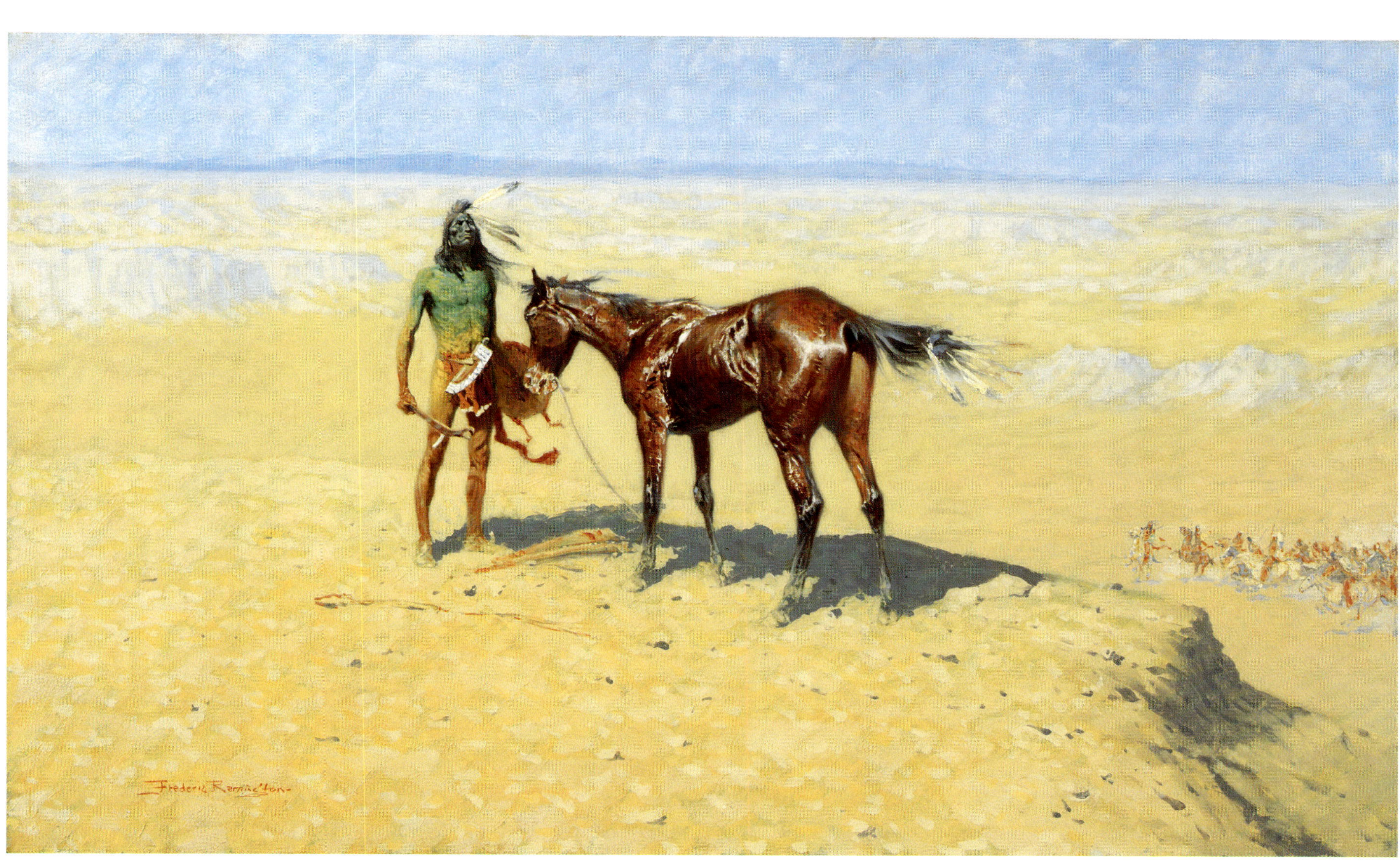
Frederic Remington

The Old Dragoons of 1850

Design copyright 1905
Bronze, lost-wax cast [#1], 1905, by Roman Bronze Works, 25⅞ x 44¼ x 17½ inches

Remington's artistic and literary successes led him to search for new subject matter in other periods of western American history. In October 1905 he instituted a new series of paintings for *Collier's* on the subject of "The Great Explorers" and was disappointed when the work was not very well received. With similar expectations, he completed work on a new bronze group that was remarkable for its complexity and degree of visual detail.

As its title indicates, *The Old Dragoons of 1850* had a historical theme, and Remington did some research to ensure accuracy in his subject. In the sculpture, two dragoons on horseback have closed in on two fleeing Indians and prepare to lock in combat. A riderless horse carrying an Indian saddle and robe runs slightly ahead of the group. Each of the dragoons wields a heavy saber, which the men dubbed "old wristbreaker," and both carry the .52-caliber Hall carbine that was standard issue in their day. The soldiers' uniforms and equipment are meant to coincide with the midcentury period, when units stationed at border posts in eastern Oklahoma and Kansas asserted a military presence on the Plains. Remington's attempts to achieve accuracy in the details of his works sometimes miss their mark; for example, the Indians are much more characteristic of the tribes the artist actually saw farther west forty years later. But the sculpture is highly effective for its dynamic visual composition.

Only three casts of this subject were made in the artist's lifetime, and each of them shows significant changes. His letters to Riccardo Bertelli at the Roman Bronze Works indicate that Remington was constantly adjusting details to improve the compositional unity and rhythm of the overall group. In the second cast, done two years after this one and now in the Metropolitan Museum of Art in New York, the artist added a buffalo robe to the leading Indian in place of the lance; unfurled overhead, it provides a visual tie-in to the rest of the group and reinforces the sense of unified movement through space. In this subject, Remington wanted the dragoons and their adversaries to convey an overwhelming sense of forward movement. The five horses are joined and supported so that some elements appear to be arrested in midair, as in the flying hooves of the rear horse. Viewed from the side, the entire group glides over the base in a low arc of headlong motion. Such effects were difficult to manage, and Remington spent long hours at the foundry attempting to perfect his increasingly difficult compositions. "If possible I guess you had better not put *Dragoons* in the fire until I see it again," he wrote Bertelli in 1905. "Those big groups have to be *just so* or it's a hard business for all hands."

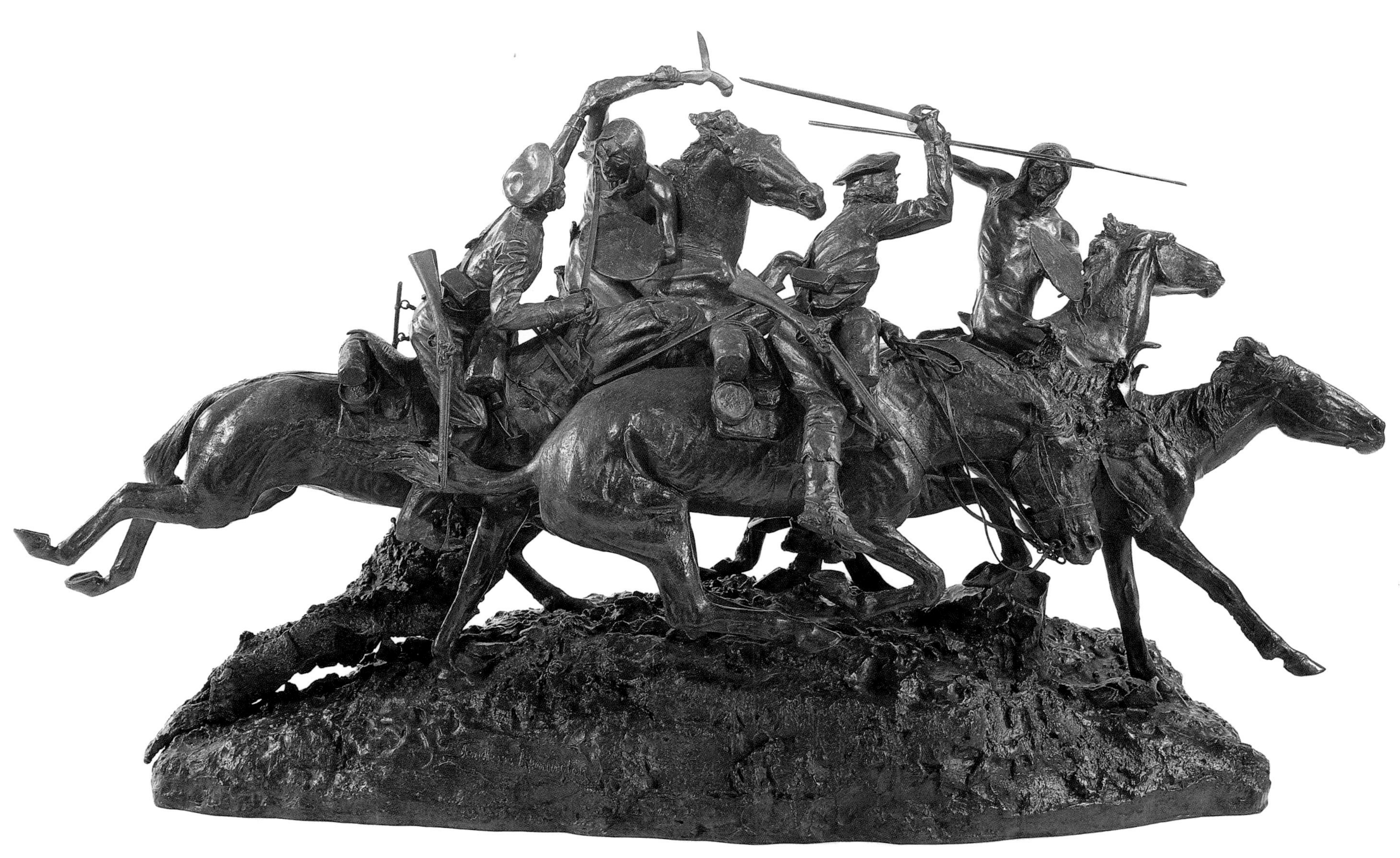

The Smoke Signal

1908, oil on canvas, 30⅛ x 48¾ inches

The Indians of the Great Plains used smoke to communicate with each other over great distances. Colonel Richard Irving Dodge, who served more than thirty-three years on the frontier and published a popular account of his experiences in 1882, accurately described the Indians' use of signal fires: "A small fire is built on which is placed damp grass, creating a large volume of smoke. As it begins to ascend a blanket is held horizontally above it, and when the space beneath is quite full, the blanket is slipped off sideways and then quickly brought back to its place. Smoke managed in this way ascends in round puffs, miniature clouds, one meaning one thing, two another." Remington has depicted this operation in his painting, *The Smoke Signal*, precisely as Dodge has described it. "A single smoke, ascending naturally, is a warning to all Indians within range of vision that there are strangers in the country," Dodge explained. "Every military command passing through an Indian country, will be preceded and flanked by these signal-smokes." The colonel also noted that a signal-fire was made on the side or the top of a high hill, away from sources of water—as the three warriors are doing in Remington's painting—to prevent the signal being confused with the smoke of a campfire.

The Indians in Remington's painting have stripped themselves to essential clothing and weapons and have tied their horses' tails with feathers—indications that they are on a war expedition. The red handprint on the white horse's rump signifies that its rider has ridden over an enemy in battle. Despite Remington's customary attention to detail, there are a few mistakes. A prominent inaccuracy is the portrayal of a woman's saddle, with its high pommel and cantle, on the braves' horses. Similarly, the warrior to the left has a single-edged knife in a tack-decorated sheath; it looks more like a woman's skinning knife than the two-edged "beaver tail" variety that should be hanging there.

Colonel Dodge marvelled at the great distances over which the Indians could observe the smoke signals; a white man would have to employ a field glass to see the same thing. He maintained that in his extensive experience few white men ever deciphered the system of smoke signals used by Indians on the Plains, and although he tried many times to obtain the secrets of the signal language from his Indian acquaintances, he was never successful. It is not generally known that in 1854 the Indian smoke-signalling methods influenced a young army lieutenant, Albert James Myers, to devise a signal-flag system for the military to use. Six years later, Myers became the first head of the newly formed Signal Corps. The cavalrymen and officers of Remington's day sometimes referred to the Corps and their method of signalling as "wig-wags" or "wig-wagging," after the manner in which the flags were handled.

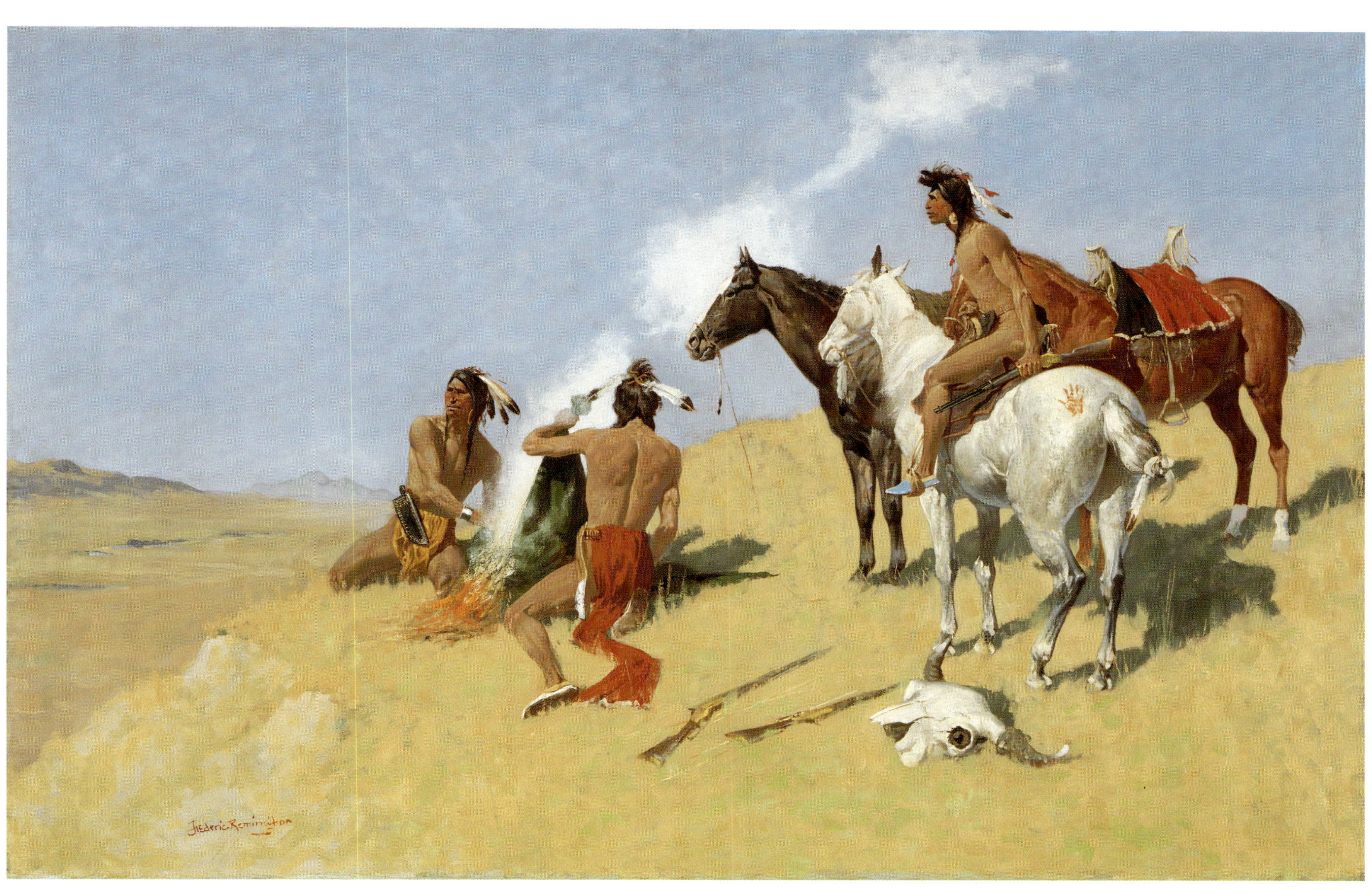
Frederic Remington

The Grass Fire

1908, oil on canvas, 27⅛ x 40⅛ inches

The last two years of Remington's life were marked by his increasing efforts to achieve recognition as a fine artist, apart from his stature as an illustrator of the American West. Although he worked harder at his paintings for *Collier's* than ever before, times were changing, and it was agreed that the artist's lucrative contract with the magazine would end in January 1909. With that prospect in mind, Remington seemed to concentrate more on exhibitions of his work at the Knoedler Galleries on Fifth Avenue, where favorable reviews and strong sales were likely to improve his acceptance among the painters in the National Academy. His show at the galleries in December 1907 produced a lukewarm reception, however, largely because the critics objected to the "crude effects" and "glaring tones" of the sunlit action scenes he had prepared for the pages of *Collier's*. On the other hand, the same critics praised some night scenes in the exhibition as "a great stride forward" in Remington's development, mainly because the works were representative of painting for its own sake and not part of the artist's career as an illustrator.

Remington continued to spend a great deal of his time studying nocturnal light effects. "Wonderful moonlight nights," he noted in his diary at one point, "tried to distinguish color in some sketches I took out of doors but it is too subtle a light and does not differentiate." It was a very busy period for him; he worked on several paintings at once, transferring them when the time came to his summer studio at Ingleneuk. A diary entry for June 5, 1908, noted that he had finished five paintings and "all of them will pass inspection I think. I am learning to use Prussian [blue] and Ultramarine in the proper way." One of the completed paintings was *The Grass Fire*, in which Prussian blue predominates in darker areas. When the painting was exhibited with eighteen others at Remington's Knoedler exhibition the following December, the press responded favorably to the artist's efforts. "Frederic Remington sounds a purely American note," a writer for the New York *Globe* proclaimed. "His color is purer, more vibrant, more telling, and his figures are more in atmosphere."

The Grass Fire was one of at least seven works that sold during the first week of the 1908 exhibition. "My show made a great hit this winter and I did pretty well," Remington wrote a friend, adding, "I am no longer an illustrator." Becoming more confident of his artistic direction, he triumphantly wrote in his diary that "I have landed among the painters, and well up too." He was anxious to enter the next phase of his productive career, and changes were under way. He put the house and studio in New Rochelle and the summer place on the Saint Lawrence River up for sale; he was building a new home and studio in Ridgefield, Connecticut, where he could be among the American impressionist painters whose work he so often viewed and admired.

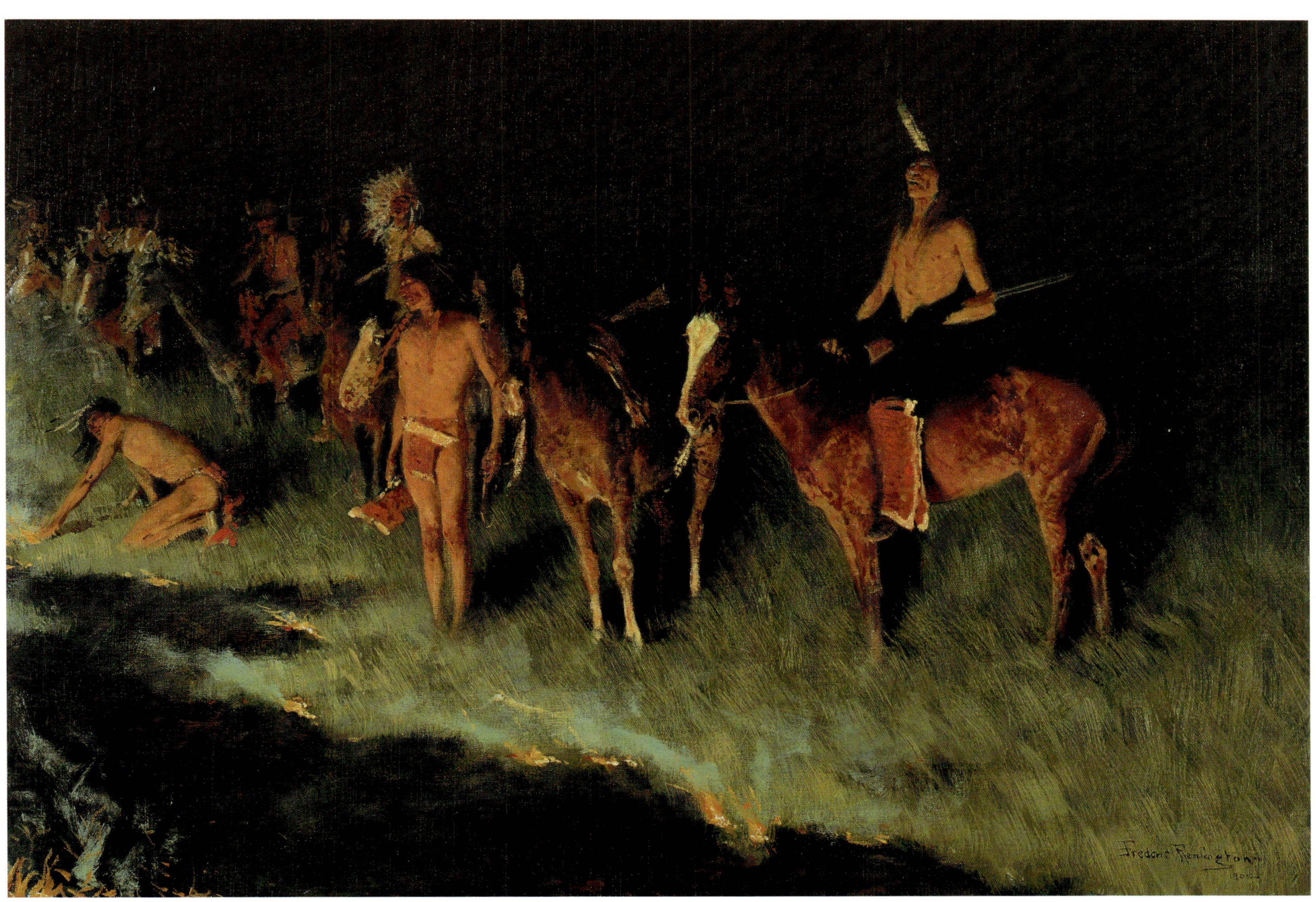

The Long-Horn Cattle Sign

1908, oil on canvas, 27⅛ x 40 inches

One of the paintings that Remington exhibited in his Knoedler Galleries exhibition of December 1908 was *The Long-Horn Cattle Sign*, an ethereal masterwork that summarizes the artist's late style. A cowboy has halted his horse to make a sign to a mounted Indian that his herd of longhorn cattle is approaching and that he would like permission to cross the reservation land. The Indian, with his closed fist over his heart, is giving the sign of acceptance. Although the subject of the picture is typical of Remington, the picture exemplifies a world of difference in the artist's late technique.

At the time he was working on the painting for *Collier's*, Remington wrote in his diary that hard outlines and direct, plein-air color would no longer be found in his work. Instead, his painting was to be "an expression of light," in the manner of the impressionist painters he was emulating. *The Long-Horn Cattle Sign* is a prime example of a work that was intended, in the artist's words, "to glow and quiver until it seems to exude the palpitating quality which light holds." Indeed, the men and horses in the painting seem to be dissolving into textures of color-laden brushstrokes, while the surrounding landscape shimmers with broad areas of vibrant tones, as if in a dream.

In many ways, *The Long-Horn Cattle Sign* conveys a true sense of Frederic Remington's West—a world that existed only in the imagination. He now used light and color to make the viewer "feel the details and not see them." What counted was the lasting visual impression.

Undoubtedly Remington was progressing rapidly towards transforming his love of western subject matter into his increasingly painterly style, but tragically, such developments were not to be. The artist's extreme obesity had caused numerous physical ailments, and after another tremendously successful showing at Knoedler's in December 1909, his luck ran out. He suffered acute stomach pains while working on several projects in his Ridgefield studio, and it was several days before doctors were asked to diagnose the artist's worsening condition. An emergency operation disclosed a ruptured appendix and the onset of an acute infection, but there was nothing to be done. On December 26, slightly past his forty-eighth birthday, Frederic Remington died. He was at the height of his artistic powers, enjoying unprecedented success at every turn.

Despite the tragic brevity of his career, Remington left an enormous legacy to American art and culture. One of the best assessments was given by a reviewer a few weeks before the artist's death. "Remington's work is splendid in its technique, epic in its imaginative qualities, and historically important," he wrote. "American history will be made more vivid than through printed pages."

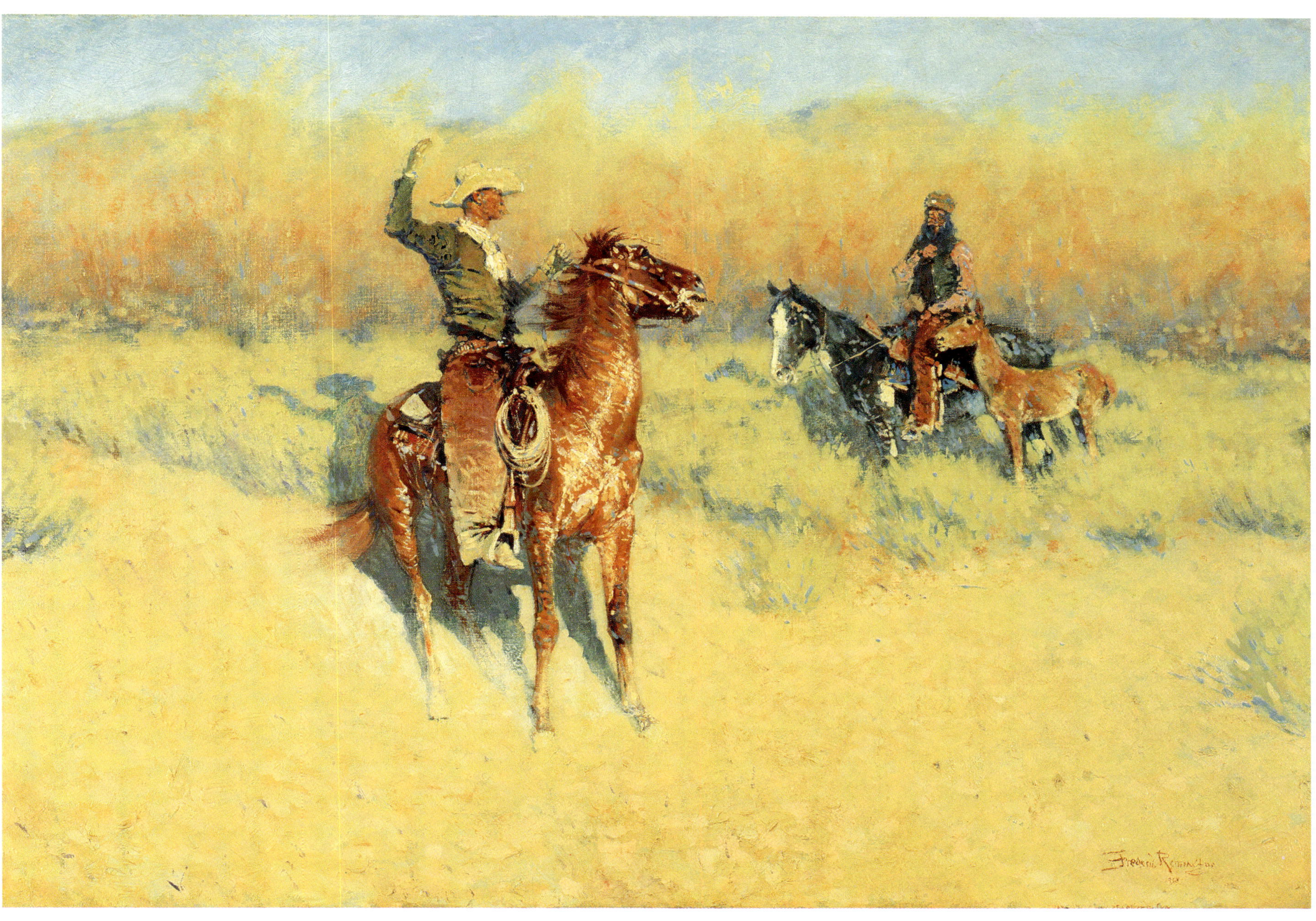

FOR FURTHER READING

Ballinger, James K. *Frederic Remington*. New York: Harry N. Abrams, Inc., 1989.

——. *Frederic Remington's Southwest*. Phoenix: Phoenix Art Museum, 1992.

Hassrick, Peter H. *Frederic Remington: Paintings, Drawings, and Sculpture in the Amon Carter Museum and Sid W. Richardson Foundation Collections*. New York: Harry N. Abrams, Inc., in association with the Amon Carter Museum, 1973.

Jussim, Estelle. *Frederic Remington, the Camera, and the Old West*. Fort Worth: Amon Carter Museum, 1983.

McCracken, Harold. *Frederic Remington: Artist of the Old West*. Philadelphia: J.B. Lippincott & Company, 1947.

Samuels, Peggy and Harold, eds. *The Collected Writings of Frederic Remington*. New York: Book Sales, Inc., 1986.

——. *Frederic Remington: A Biography*. New York: Doubleday & Company, 1982.

——. *Remington: The Complete Prints*. New York: Crown Publishers, Inc., 1990.

Shapiro, Michael Edward. *Cast and Recast: The Sculpture of Frederic Remington*. Washington, D.C.: Smithsonian Institution Press for the National Museum of American Art, 1981.

——, and Peter H. Hassrick. *Frederic Remington: The Masterworks*. New York: Harry N. Abrams, Inc., in association with the Saint Louis Art Museum and the Buffalo Bill Historical Center, 1988.

Splete, Allen P. and Marilyn D. *Frederic Remington—Selected Letters*. New York: Abbeville Press, 1988.

Vorpahl, Ben Merchant. *Frederic Remington and the West; With the Eye of the Mind*. Austin: University of Texas Press, 1978.

——. *My Dear Wister: The Frederic Remington-Owen Wister Letters*. Palo Alto: American West Publishing Company, 1972.